D1373279

# Academic Vocabulary Practice
## Grade 4

**Credits**

Content Editor: Shirley Pearson

Copy Editor: Julie B. Killian

Visit *carsondellosa.com* for correlations to Common Core, state, national, and Canadian provincial standards.

Carson-Dellosa Publishing, LLC

PO Box 35665

Greensboro, NC 27425 USA

carsondellosa.com

ISBN 978-1-4838-1121-5

01-135141151

# Table of Contents

# Introduction

## The Academic Vocabulary Practice Series

Research shows that a firm knowledge of academic vocabulary is one of the strongest indicators of a student's success in the content areas. Academic Vocabulary Practice is a series that provides students with the resources they need to build crucial vocabulary skills for success in school. The series promotes and supports literacy in: math, science, technology, language arts, social studies, geography, civics and economics, and art. The reproducible pages are designed to give students extra practice using academic vocabulary. The word lists focus on subject-specific words that often challenge students because they may rarely encounter these words in everyday use.

The books align with the Common Core State Standards by offering systematic practice and usage of many of the academic and domain-specific words and phrases. Teaching vocabulary to meet the Common Core State Standards is an essential component of any standards-based curriculum.

## Reproducible Pages in This Book

This book presents 200+ subject-specific words that are organized by content area. Ample opportunity is given to help students learn and connect with the vocabulary in a variety of ways.

- The *Vocabulary Four Square* on page 4 is an essential organizer that helps students learn new words by stating word meanings in their own words, drawing pictures to represent the words, engaging with peers in word discussions, and creating context for words.

- The *Explore a Word* activities let students focus on one word at a time to create associations.

- The *Compare Words* activities show students how two or more related words are alike and different in meaning.

- The *Make Connections* pages help students understand the relationships between words that are commonly presented together.

- The *Play with Words* activities provide review in a more playful but effective learning format.

## Special Features

The *Game Ideas and Suggestions* section includes ideas for using the flash cards (offered online) and game templates for small group or whole group activities. The *Student Dictionary* pages are organized by content area and support the activity pages in each section.

## Online Support

To further enhance student learning, the 200+ vocabulary words are available in flash card format online at *activities.carsondellosa.com*. These will provide opportunities for additional practice and other peer activities.

# Vocabulary Four Square

Use the Vocabulary Four Square to practice new words in this book.

| What I Think the Word Means | Picture |
|---|---|
| **Word** _____ | |
| What My Friend Thinks the Word Means | Synonyms |
| | Antonyms |
| Sentence | |

# Important Math
# Words You Need to Know

Use this list to keep track of how well you know the new words.

0 = Don't Know          1 = Know It Somewhat          2 = Know It Well

___ bar graph                    ___ mixed number

___ center                       ___ mode

___ centimeter                   ___ number sentence

___ circle graph                 ___ operation

___ circumference                ___ percent

___ common denominator           ___ plane

___ convert                      ___ point of intersection

___ cube                         ___ prism

___ cubic unit                   ___ probability

___ cylinder                     ___ proper fraction

___ diameter                     ___ pyramid

___ equation                     ___ radius

___ equivalent fractions         ___ range

___ face                         ___ rounding

___ factor                       ___ solid

___ frequency table              ___ vertical axis

___ horizontal axis              ___ volume

___ improper fraction

___ inequality

___ kilometer

___ line graph

___ mean

___ median

Name _____

# Explore a Word

Read the paragraph. Think about the meaning of the **bold** word.

> Imagine tossing a penny into the air. The chance that it will land heads up is the same as the chance that it will land tails up. An even chance means that the **probability** is "one-half" or "$\frac{1}{2}$."

1. What do you think the word means? Write your idea.

   **probability:** _____

   _____

2. Write a sentence with the word **probability**. Show what it means.

   _____

   _____

3. Check the meaning of **probability** in the Student Dictionary.

4. If your sentence in step 2 matches the meaning, put a ✓ after it. If your sentence does not match the meaning, write a better sentence.

   _____

   _____

5. Make a simple drawing to show the meaning of **probability**.

# Compare Words

Look at the pictures and read the captions. Think about the meaning of each **bold** word. Then, check the Student Dictionary.

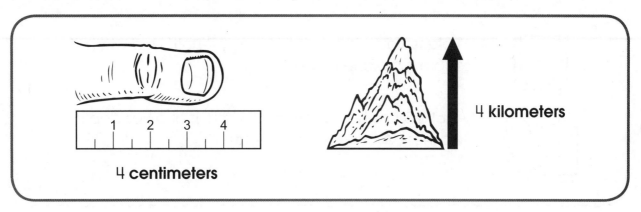

4 **centimeters**

4 **kilometers**

Complete the chart with your own ideas.

| Length or Distance | Example |
|---|---|
| 1 centimeter (cm) | thickness of a picture book |
| 5 kilometers (km) | |
| 10 cm | |
| 10 km | |
| | distance between school and home |
| | length of a pencil |

 # Word Alert!

A prefix is a word part added before a word. Measurement words often have prefixes.

| Prefix | Word | Meaning |
|---|---|---|
| *centi-* means "one hundredth" | *meter* | *centimeter* means "one-hundredth (0.01) of a meter" |
| *kilo-* means "one thousand" | *meter* | *kilometer* means "one thousand (1,000) meters" |

A liter bottle holds about 4 cups of water.

1.  How much is in a centiliter? _____

2.  How much is in a kiloliter? _____

# Compare Words

Read the sentences. Think about the meaning of each **bold** word. Then, check the
Student Dictionary.

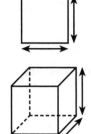 A **plane** figure is flat and has only length and width. A
square is a plane figure.

A **solid** figure has length and width. It also has depth, or
thickness. A cube is a solid figure.

Label each figure with the word *plane* or *solid*.

1.

_____

2.

_____

3.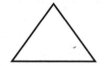

_____

4.

_____

5.

_____

6.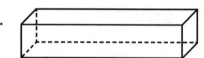

_____

# 🔍 Look It Up!

Each meaning of a word is numbered in a dictionary entry. Look up the word *plane* in a
classroom dictionary. Write the meaning that fits with this page.

_____

_____

Name _____

# Compare Words

Look at the examples and read the captions. Think about the meaning of each **bold** word. Then, check the Student Dictionary.

| $2 \times 5 = 10$ | $2 \times 5 > 8$ | $10 \times 2 < 30$ |
|---|---|---|
| **equation** ("equal to") | **inequality** ("greater than") | **inequality** ("less than") |

How are equations and inequalities alike? How are they different? Complete the chart. List at least two ways they are alike. List as many differences as possible.

| Equation | Both | Inequality |
|---|---|---|
|  |  |  |

## ❗ Word Alert!

The words *equation* and *inequality* share the letters *equ*. This group of letters comes from a Latin root that means "even" or "level."

Many other words, such as *equal* and *equator*, share this Latin root. With a partner, take turns explaining what each word means. What is alike about all the meanings?

_____

_____

# Make Connections

Read the paragraph. Think about the meaning of each **bold** word. Then, check the Student Dictionary.

> A math **operation** is any action, such as adding or dividing, that involves numbers. One operation is **rounding**. For example, the amount $4.59 is rounded up to $4.60 or to $5.00. $4.32 is rounded down to $4.30 or to $4.00.

Pretend that you are a teacher. Complete the dialogue with the correct answers.

1. Student: I know that adding, dividing, and rounding are math operations. What are some other math operations?

   Teacher: _____

2. Student: When should I use rounding?

   Teacher: _____

   _____

3. Student: How do I round 627 to the nearest ten?

   Teacher: _____

   _____

4. Student: How do I round 627 to the nearest hundred?

   Teacher: _____

   _____

Take turns reading the dialogue with a partner. Are there any changes you should make to it? If so, show those changes above.

# Make Connections

Look at the pictures and read the captions. Think about the meaning of each **bold** word. Then, check the Student Dictionary.

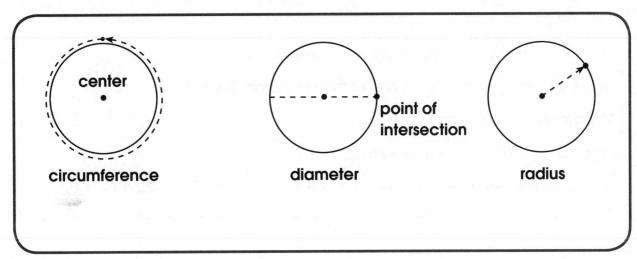

center

circumference

diameter

point of intersection

radius

Circle *Yes* or *No* for each question. Write your reason on the line.

1.  Is the diameter of a circle half the length of the radius?  Yes  No

   _____

2.  Does a radius touch the center of a circle?  Yes  No

   _____

3.  Do the radius and the circumference intersect at the center?  Yes  No

   _____

4.  Does this picture show diameter?  Yes  No

   _____

5.  Does this picture show a radius?    Yes  No

   _____

6.  Could a square have a circumference?  Yes  No

   _____

# Make Connections

Read the sentences. Think about the meaning of each **bold** term. Then, check the Student Dictionary.

The fractions $\frac{3}{4}$, $\frac{9}{12}$, and $\frac{75}{100}$ are **equivalent fractions**.

The fractions $\frac{1}{4}$ and $\frac{3}{4}$ have a **common denominator** of 4.

A **percent** has 100 in the denominator.

$\frac{5}{100} = 0.05 = 5\%$;   $\frac{75}{100} = 0.75 = 75\%$.

In the **number sentence** $3 \times 5 = 15$, the numbers 3 and 5 are **factors** of 15.

Follow the directions to draw or write.

1. Draw a picture to show a cookie cut in half. Label one piece $\frac{1}{2}$. Label the other piece with an equivalent fraction.

2. Draw a square. Shade 25 percent of it. Draw stripes in 75 percent of it.

3. Fractions can be added only if they have a common denominator. Write a number sentence to show what that means.

_____

4. The number 1 is a factor of every whole number. Write two number sentences to show what that means.

_____

 **Challenge!**

Change two equivalent fractions into a fraction with the lowest common denominator. Show your work.

# Make Connections

Read the paragraph. Think about the meaning of each **bold** term. Then, check the Student Dictionary.

> The fraction $\frac{2}{3}$ is a **proper fraction**. The fraction $\frac{4}{3}$ is an **improper fraction**. That's because $\frac{4}{3}$ can be **converted** to the **mixed number** $1\frac{1}{3}$.

Follow the directions to draw or write.

1.  Draw a picture of 2 pizzas. Draw a line through each pizza to cut each in half.

    How many half-pizzas do you have altogether? _____

    Write this as an improper fraction of the 2 full pizzas. _____

2.  Shade 3 of the pizza halves. What fraction of the 2 pizzas is shaded?

    Write your answer as an improper fraction of the 2 full pizzas. _____

    Convert your answer to a mixed number. _____

    Why do you think this is called a *mixed number*?

    _____

    _____

3.  Convert the improper fraction $\frac{7}{3}$ to a mixed number. _____

4.  Convert the mixed number $1\frac{3}{4}$ to an improper fraction. _____

 **Challenge!**

The word *convert* means to change something so that it can be used in a different way. Can you think of a situation when you would want to use an improper fraction instead of a mixed number in an equation?

_____

_____

Name _____

# Make Connections

Read the paragraph and look at the pictures. Think about the meaning of each **bold** term. Then, check the Student Dictionary.

A **cube** is an example of a solid figure. A **pyramid**, a **prism**, and a **cylinder** are other solid figures. The sides of a solid figure are called **faces**. The space inside of a solid figure is called the **volume**. Volume is measured in **cubic units** such as cubic inches, cubic feet, and cubic meters.

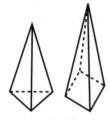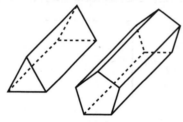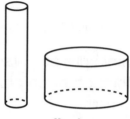

| pyramids | prisms | cylinders |

Complete each sentence with a vocabulary word.

1. Each face of a pyramid is the shape of a _____.

2. Each face of a prism has _____ sides.

3. Each base of a cylinder is the shape of a _____.

4. Multiply the length by the width by the depth to find the _____ of a box.

5. One common object with a volume of about 8 cubic feet is a _____.

Draw a cube. Label its length, width, and depth. Write a sentence about it using the words *cubic units* and *volume*.

_____

_____

_____

_____

Academic Vocabulary Practice • Grade 4 • CD-104809

# Make Connections

Read the paragraphs. Think about the meaning of each **bold** term. Then, check the Student Dictionary.

A **bar graph** contains a lot of information. A **frequency table** is similar to a bar graph. They both compare amounts. The labels on the horizontal axis identify the object being measured or counted. The labels on the vertical axis show how much or how many.

So, what kind of information does a frequency table hold?

- **range**—The difference between the biggest and smallest results.
- **mode**—The most frequently occurring result.
- **median**—The middle result.
- **mean**—The average result.

Look at the bar graph. Label the horizontal axis and the vertical axis with your own ideas. For each label on the horizontal axis, draw a rectangle to show how many pets. Then, write a sentence to explain what the graph shows. Use the term *bar graph* in your sentence.

**Number of Pets**

_____

_____

_____

_____

Look at your bar graph. Think of it as a frequency table. Answer the questions. Then, explain how you calculated each answer.

1. What is the *range* of data? _____

   Explain: _____

2. What is the *mode*? _____

   Explain: _____

3. What is the *median*? _____

   Explain: _____

4. What is the *mean*? _____

   Explain: _____

# Make Connections

Read the paragraphs. Think about the meaning of each **bold** term. Then, check the Student Dictionary.

A **circle graph** is sometimes called a pie chart. It is broken into sections that show the parts of a whole, just like the slices of a pie.

A **line graph** shows changes over time. The labels on the **horizontal axis** show units of time such as days or months. The labels on the **vertical axis** show how much or how many.

Look at the circle graph. Label the sections with your own ideas. Then, write a sentence to explain what the graph shows. Use the term *circle graph* in your sentence.

**Favorite Outdoor Activities
of 150 Students**

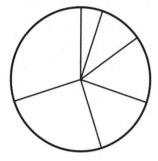

_____
_____
_____
_____
_____

Look at the line graph. Label the horizontal axis and the vertical axis with your own ideas. Draw a line on the graph. Then, write a sentence to explain what the graph shows. Use the term *line graph* in your sentence.

**How Much Did I Read This Week?**

_____
_____
_____
_____
_____

# Play with Words

## Code Words

Choose the word or words that complete each sentence. Circle the letter.

1.  A wheel has a ___.
    d   median
    e   circumference
    f   probability

2.  Find the sum of this ___.
    q   intersect
    r   face
    s   equation

3.  Three is a ___ of six.
    t   factor
    u   mixed number
    v   convert

4.  One-hundredth is a small ___.
    i   probability
    j   operation
    k   frequency table

5.  A sphere is a ___ figure.
    l   plane
    m   solid
    n   radius

6.  Measure your height in ___.
    a   centimeters
    b   modes
    c   diameters

7.  One-half is equal to 50 ___.
    s   proper fractions
    t   percent
    u   cubic units

8.  The ___ shows a steep drop in temperature.
    e   line graph
    f   circle graph
    g   mean

Write the circled letters in order. You will find a word that tells what people often do to determine how much or how many.

_____

# Play with Words

## Letter by Letter

Choose the word that fits with each clue. Write it letter by letter. Some letters will be inside circles.

| cubic | cylinder | inequality | kilometer |
|-------|----------|------------|-----------|
| prism | pyramid | radius | rounding |

1.     — ⬤ — — — — — —

2. 43<u>6</u> → 440    — ⬤ — — — — —

3. A balloon holds _____ centimeters of air.    — — ⬤ — — —

4.     — — ⬤ — — —

5. a 10-_____ race    — ⬤ — — — — —

6.     — — — — — ⬤ —

7. 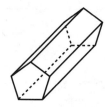    — — ⬤ — —

8. 3 × 4 > 5 × 2    — — — — — — — — ⬤ —

Write the circled letters in order to find a message.

— — — —   — — — —   — — !

# Play with Words

Unscramble the letters to write a math term that fits with each picture or example. The term will be a compound word.

1.

iccerl       pargh

_____

2. $\frac{1}{4}$, $\frac{2}{8}$, $\frac{25}{100}$

quanveilet      noictrafs

_____

3. $\frac{1}{7}$, $\frac{3}{7}$, $\frac{5}{7}$

moncom      ratnonimoed

_____

4.

inel      garph

_____

5.

zorhitloan      sixa

_____

6.

trelicav      ixas

_____

# Round It

Draw a circle with a radius of about 2 centimeters. Use this equation and rounding to help you measure: 1 inch = 2.54 centimeters. Shade about 20 percent of your plane figure to make it look like a solid figure. Then, add any details you like.

# Important Science Words You Need to Know

Use this list to keep track of how well you know the new words.

0 = Don't Know          1 = Know It Somewhat          2 = Know It Well

___ carnivore

___ chemical energy

___ circuit

___ closed circuit

___ conductor

___ consumer

___ crater

___ crust

___ decomposer

___ earthquake

___ electric current

___ electric energy

___ energy

___ erosion

___ erupt

___ fault

___ food chain

___ fossil

___ frequency

___ herbivore

___ igneous

___ inner core

___ insulator

___ intensity

___ lava

___ light energy

___ magma

___ mantle

___ metamorphic

___ mineral

___ omnivore

___ open circuit

___ organism

___ outer core

___ pitch

___ producer

___ rock cycle

___ sedimentary

___ sound energy

___ transform

___ vibrate

___ volcano

___ volume

___ wavelength

___ weathering

# Explore a Word

Read the paragraph. Think about the meaning of the **bold** word.

> Long ago, animals walked across a muddy shore. The mud hardened, and the animals' tracks remained. Today, scientists study these tracks and other **fossils** to learn about prehistoric life.

1. What do you think the word means? Write your idea.

   **fossil:** _____

   _____

2. Write a sentence with the word **fossil**. Show what it means.

   _____

   _____

3. Check the meaning of **fossil** in the Student Dictionary.

4. If your sentence in question 2 matches the meaning, put a ✓ after it. If your sentence does not match the meaning, write a better sentence.

   _____

   _____

5. Make a simple drawing to show the meaning of **fossil**.

# Compare Words

Read the paragraph. Think about the meaning of each **bold** word. Then, check the Student Dictionary.

> Heat, cold, rain, wind, and living things all act on rocks and soil. Heat and cold can crack a rock in half. Plant roots can cause a rock to break into smaller pieces. These kinds of changes are called **weathering**. Water can also carry rocks and soil from one place to another. Wind can blow soil to new places too. The movement of rocks and soil is called **erosion**.

Read each sentence. Is it an example of erosion or weathering? Circle the answer.

1. A river carries soil all the way to the ocean.                          erosion        weathering

2. A tree grows from a small crack in a rock,
   making the crack wider.                                                 erosion        weathering

3. Rain washes soil and small rocks down
   a mountainside.                                                         erosion        weathering

4. Hot summers and icy winters cause a
   boulder to split apart.                                                 erosion        weathering

5. Farmers worry about a flood that is washing
   good soil away.                                                         erosion        weathering

Look at this picture of a mountain. Add arrows and captions to tell about weathering and erosion.

# Make Connections

Read the paragraph. Think about the meaning of each **bold** term. Then, check the Student Dictionary.

> Flip the switch, and an **electric current** is on the move! It flows through a wire to the lightbulb and then back again. When **electric energy** is **transformed** into **light energy**, the light turns on. This path is called a **circuit**. A metal wire is a good **conductor** of electricity. Plastic around the wire is a good **insulator**.

This is a picture of an **open circuit**. The battery contains **chemical energy**, but the lightbulb will not light! Write instructions for how to create a **closed circuit** to turn it on. Use the vocabulary words in your instructions.

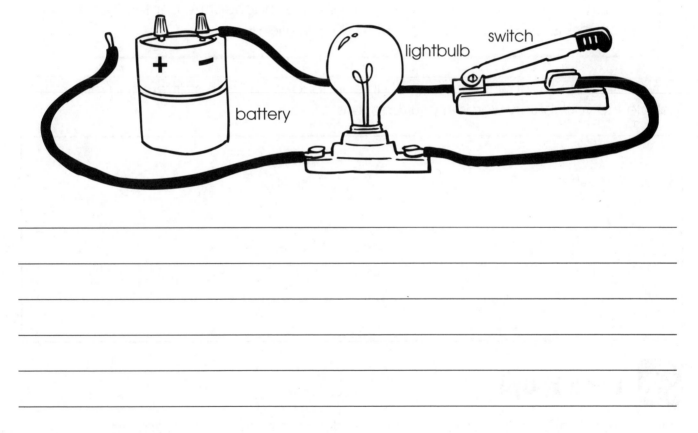

battery    lightbulb    switch

_____

_____

_____

_____

_____

_____

## 🔍 Look It Up!

The word *conductor* has more than one meaning. Use a classroom dictionary to find three meanings of the word. On a separate sheet of paper, draw three pictures to show the different meanings.

# Make Connections

Read the paragraphs. Think about the meaning of each **bold** word. Then, check the Student Dictionary.

> Imagine drilling a hole to the center of Earth. What would you find? First, you would drill through the **crust**. This outer layer may be up to 40 kilometers (25 miles) thick. The crust and the uppermost part of the **mantle** beneath it are broken into giant plates. The edges of some plates may slide against each other to form a **fault**, or break. **Earthquakes** happen along faults.
>
> Earth's plates move because they lie on super-hot rocks that flow like thick liquid. This molten rock makes up the rest of the mantle, which is about 2,900 kilometers (1,800 miles) thick.
>
> Keep drilling. First, youll will pass through Earth's thick **outer core** and then through its **inner core**. Finally, you will have reached the center, that is, if your drill is 6,400 kilometers (about 4,000 miles) long!

Draw a diagram to show the impact of an earthquake on Earth's different layers. Include the vocabulary words in your captions.

 **Look It Up!**

Science words often have special meanings, different from the everyday meanings of the same words. Look up the vocabulary words in a classroom dictionary. Write the number and the meaning that fit with science.

1. crust _____

2. fault _____

3. mantle _____

# Make Connections

Read the paragraphs. Think about the meaning of each **bold** word. Then, check the Student Dictionary.

> Molten rock from below Earth's crust is called **magma**. When magma **erupts** from a **volcano**, it shoots out as red-hot **lava**, cinders, and ash. This eruption creates a **crater**.

Use the vocabulary words in captions to label this diagram.

 ## Word Alert!

The root -*rupt* comes from a Latin word that means "to break." Use the word *break* to describe each word below.

1. erupt _____

2. disrupt _____

3. interrupt _____

4. rupture _____

# Make Connections

Look at the diagram. Think about the meaning of each **bold** term. Then, check the Student Dictionary.

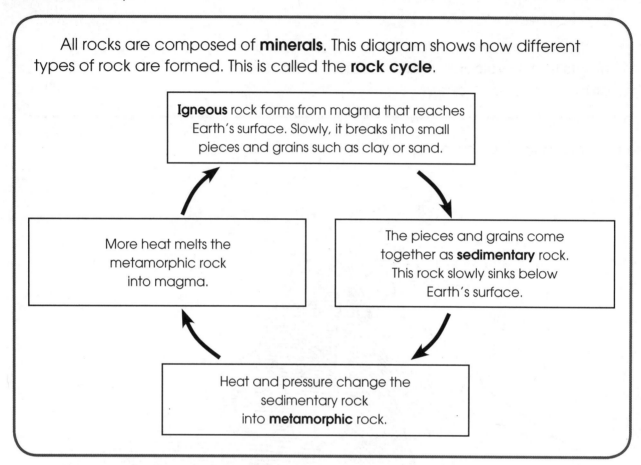

All rocks are composed of **minerals**. This diagram shows how different types of rock are formed. This is called the **rock cycle**.

**Igneous** rock forms from magma that reaches Earth's surface. Slowly, it breaks into small pieces and grains such as clay or sand.

More heat melts the metamorphic rock into magma.

The pieces and grains come together as **sedimentary** rock. This rock slowly sinks below Earth's surface.

Heat and pressure change the sedimentary rock into **metamorphic** rock.

Underline the correct ending to each sentence.

1.  You would expect to find igneous rock
    A.   on the slopes of a volcano.
    B.   on land that was once a lake bottom.

2.  An example of sedimentary rock is
    A.   sandstone, formed from layers of sand.
    B.   granite, formed from magma beneath Earth's surface.

3.  An example of metamorphic rock is
    A.   shale, formed from layers of clay.
    B.   slate, formed from buried shale.

4.  A complete rock cycle probably takes
    A.   millions of years.
    B.   hundreds of years.

# Make Connections

Look at the diagram. Read the paragraph. Think about the meaning of each **bold** word. Then, check the Student Dictionary.

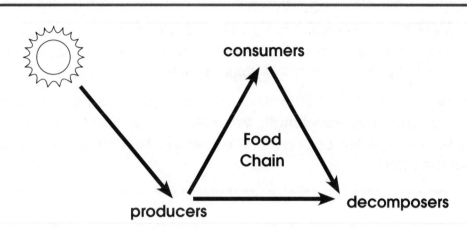

All **organisms** need **energy** to survive. Plants get energy from the sun. **Herbivores** and **omnivores** eat plants. **Carnivores** and omnivores eat other animals. Fungi and bacteria decompose everything, returning energy back to the soil. This is called the Food Chain.

Complete each sentence with a vocabulary word. Use each word only once.

1. _____ eat both plants and animals.

2. The cycle of energy within an ecosystem is called the _____.

3. Predators such as polar bears are _____.

4. Herbivores, carnivores, and omnivores are all _____.

5. Plant-eating animals are called _____.

6. _____ break down plant and animal matter.

7. Plants are _____.

8. Plants convert the sun's _____ into food.

9. _____ are living things.

 # Challenge!

Think of a carnivore. On a separate sheet of paper, draw its food chain. How many steps does it take for the sun's energy to return to the soil in your carnivore's food chain?

# Make Connections

Read the paragraphs. Think about the meaning of each **bold** word. Then, check the Student Dictionary.

> When something **vibrates**, it produces **sound energy**. The energy moves along in waves. The **intensity** of the waves is a measure of their power. The higher the intensity, the greater the **volume**, or loudness, of the sound.
>
> Sound also has **pitch**, or highness or lowness. The distance between any two waves is called the **wavelength**. Wavelengths are shorter in something that vibrates very quickly, or at a high **frequency**. The higher the frequency, the higher the pitch.

Complete each sentence. Include the vocabulary word in your answer.

1.  intensity
    I hit the drum as hard as I could, but _____

    _____ .

2.  frequency
    When I want to play a high note, I _____

    _____ .

3.  vibrate
    When I tap a glass with a spoon, _____

    _____ .

4.  volume
    I blew gently into the horn because I _____

    _____ .

5.  pitch
    Our music teacher sings in a voice that has _____

    _____ .

6.  wavelength
    Some animals can hear sounds that we cannot, because they _____

    _____ .

## Play with Words

### Code Words

Choose the word or words that complete each sentence. Circle the letter.

1. Miners dig deep into Earth's ___.
   - **t** minerals
   - **u** magma
   - **v** crust

2. The ___ of sound is its loudness.
   - **n** frequency
   - **o** intensity
   - **p** conductor

3. Dinosaur bones are examples of ___.
   - **j** erosion
   - **k** carnivores
   - **l** fossils

4. Lava spilled out of the ___ volcano.
   - **c** erupting
   - **d** mantle
   - **e** metamorphic

5. Hit a drum to make it ___.
   - **a** vibrate
   - **b** volume
   - **c** pitch

6. An electric current will not flow through ___.
   - **m** a circuit
   - **n** an insulator
   - **o** a conductor

7. A battery contains ___ energy.
   - **h** light
   - **i** chemical
   - **j** transform

8. Close the ___ to turn on the light.
   - **a** mantle
   - **b** food chain
   - **c** circuit

Write the circled letters in order. You will find a word that describes rocks, a mountain, an island, or a fiery temper!

_____

*Academic Vocabulary Practice • Grade 4 • CD-104809*

**29**

# Play with Words

## Letter by Letter

Choose the word that fits with each clue. Write it letter by letter. Some letters will be inside circles.

| circuit | crater | crust | decomposers | energy |
|---------|--------|-------|-------------|--------|
| erosion | igneous | lava | organism | vibrate |

1. This can pour from a volcano.  ___ ⬭ ___ ___

2. This floats on Earth's mantle.  ⬭ ___ ___ ___ ___

3. This is anything that is alive.  ⬭ ___ ___ ___ ___ ___ ___

4. This is food.  ___ ⬭ ___ ___ ___ ___

5. These replace nutrients in the soil.  ⬭ ___ ___ ___ ___ ___ ___ ___ ___ ___ ___

6. An electric current flows through this.  ___ ___ ___ ___ ⬭ ___ ___

7. This is a hole left after a volcano erupts.  ⬭ ___ ___ ___ ___ ___

8. Plucked strings do this.  ___ ___ ___ ___ ___ ___ ⬭

9. This describes volcanic rock.  ___ ___ ___ ___ ⬭ ___ ___

10. This leads to soil in new places.  ___ ⬭ ___ ___ ___ ___ ___

Write the circled letters in order. You will find the answer to this riddle. *How are an electric current and a group of musicians alike?*

Each needs ___    ___ ___ ___ ___ ___ ___ ___ ___ ___.

# Play with Words

## If So, Then Write

Read the instructions. Then, write the correct letter in the blank. When you finish, you should have spelled a science word.

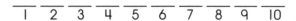

$$\overline{\quad}\ \overline{\quad}\ \overline{\quad}\ \overline{\quad}\ \overline{\quad}\ \overline{\quad}\ \overline{\quad}\ \overline{\quad}\ \overline{\quad}\ \overline{\quad}$$
1  2  3  4  5  6  7  8  9  10

1. If lava comes from magma, write *E* on blank 1. If lava comes from fossils, write *T* on blank 1.

2. If producers eat consumers, write *A* on blank 2. If consumers eat producers, write *X* on blank 2.

3. If faults occur on Earth's crust, write *P* on blank 3. If faults are the result of weathering, write *N* on blank 3.

4. If an electric current flows through an insulator, write *K* on blank 4. If an electric current flows through a conductor, write *E* on blank 4.

5. If erosion is part of the rock cycle, write *R* on blank 5. If erosion has nothing to do with the rock cycle, write *G* on blank 5.

6. If electric energy flows successfully through an open circuit, write *O* on blank 6. If electric energy flows successfully through a closed circuit, write *I* on blank 6.

7. If a wavelength has to do with how loud a sound is, write *Y* on blank 7. If a wavelength has to do with how high a sound is, write *M* on blank 7.

8. If a vibrating object has a circuit, write *B* on blank 8. If a vibrating object has a pitch, write *E* on blank 8.

9. If a volcano holds magma, write *N* on blank 9. If a volcano holds a fault, write *P* on blank 9.

10. If the inner core is closer to Earth's center than the outer core, write *T* on blank 10. If the inner core is farther from Earth's center than the outer core, write *S* on blank 10.

# Important Technology Words You Need to Know

Use this list to keep track of how well you know the new words.

0 = Don't Know      1 = Know It Somewhat      2 = Know It Well

___ complex machine                 ___ renewable

___ conservation                    ___ resistance

___ CPU                             ___ simple machine

___ data                            ___ solar energy

___ effort

___ electronic

___ force

___ fossil fuel

___ friction

___ fulcrum

___ geothermal energy

___ gravity

___ icon

___ lever

___ load

___ mechanical

___ memory

___ menu

___ motion

___ multimedia

___ natural resource

___ nonrenewable

___ processor

Name _____

# Explore a Word

Read the paragraph. Think about the meaning of the **bold** word. Then, check the Student Dictionary.

> The prefix *multi-* means "many." The word *media* means "more than one medium." A medium is a way of giving information or communicating with the public. **Multimedia** is a combination of text, sound, graphics, animations, photos, video, and other media. Multimedia is computer-controlled. Video games are one form of multimedia.

Complete the web to show your understanding of the word *multimedia*.

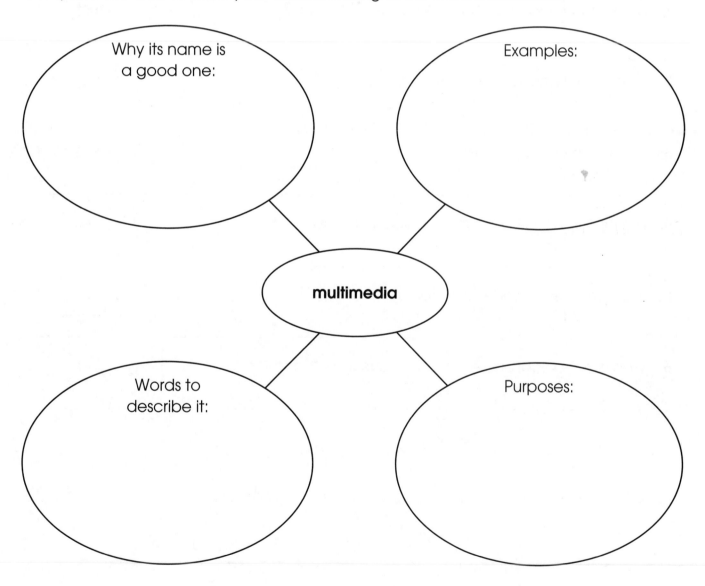

# Compare Words

Read the paragraph. Think about the meaning of each **bold** word. Then, check the Student Dictionary.

> A **mechanical** device, such as a washing machine, has moving parts. A mechanical device may be powered by electricity. Today, many machines also have electronic parts. These **electronic** parts use electric signals on tiny circuits.

Circle *Yes* or *No* for each question. Write your reason on the line.

**1.** Is an electric can opener a mechanical device?      Yes    No

_____

**2.** Does a cell phone have electronic parts?      Yes    No

_____

**3.** Is a TV an electronic device?      Yes    No

_____

**4.** Is a laptop computer a mechanical invention?      Yes    No

_____

**5.** Were the first airplanes electronic?      Yes    No

_____

**6.** Can mechanical and electronic parts work together?      Yes    No

_____

# Make Connections

Read the paragraph. Think about the meaning of each **bold** word. Then, check the Student Dictionary.

> **Force** causes new **motion** or a change in existing motion. Different kinds of forces cause objects to move in different ways. Imagine you are on your bike at the top of a hill. The force of **gravity** pulls you down the hill. Then, you are on flat ground. If you do not pedal, what will happen? The force of **friction** will cause your bike to slow down, and your motion will come to a stop.

Read each sentence. Is it an example of gravity or friction? Circle the answer.

1. Things fall down, not up.          gravity     friction

2. A rolling ball stops rolling.          gravity     friction

3. Car tires grip the road without slipping.       gravity     friction

4. The planets stay in orbit around the sun.      gravity     friction

5. Heavy birds flap their wings hard to get off the ground.    gravity     friction

 **Challenge!**

Imagine jumping into a pool or a lake. Picture walking through waist-high water. Use the words *friction* and *gravity* to describe what you imagine.

_____

_____

_____

_____

# Make Connections

Name _____

Look at the pictures and read captions. Read the numbered paragraphs. Think about the meaning of each **bold** word. Then, check the Student Dictionary.

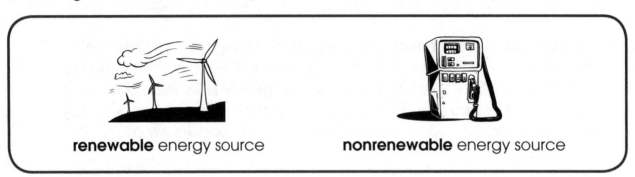

renewable energy source        nonrenewable energy source

Circle the word in parentheses that completes each paragraph.

1. Much of our electric power is made by burning coal, oil, and natural gas. But, these **fossil fuels** need millions of years to develop. That is why it is important to practice energy **conservation** to save energy. Fossil fuels are a **natural resource**. They are not made by people but occur naturally. Fossil fuels are (renewable, nonrenewable) sources of energy.

2. The sun sends energy to Earth in the forms of light and heat. People have learned how to use **solar energy** to make electric power. But, the methods for using this (renewable, nonrenewable) source are costly.

3. In some parts of the world, magma reaches up through Earth's crust. This heat from inside Earth, or **geothermal energy**, can be turned into electric power. Geothermal energy is a (renewable, nonrenewable) source.

 **Word Alert!**

The words *renewable* and *nonrenewable* contain prefixes and suffixes added to the same root word. Break apart the two words to complete squares 1-4 on the chart.

| Prefix | Prefix | Root Word | Suffix | Definition |
|---|---|---|---|---|
| | *re-* means "again" | 1. | *-able* means "able to be" | *renewable* means "able to be made new again" |
| *non-* means "not" | 2. | *new* | 3. | 4. |

     Academic Vocabulary Practice • Grade 4 • CD-104809

# Make Connections

Read the paragraph and look at the diagram. Think about the meaning of each **bold** word. Then, check the Student Dictionary.

A machine is something that helps make work easier for people. A **simple machine** performs one task. A **complex machine** is made up of many simple machines and performs complex tasks.

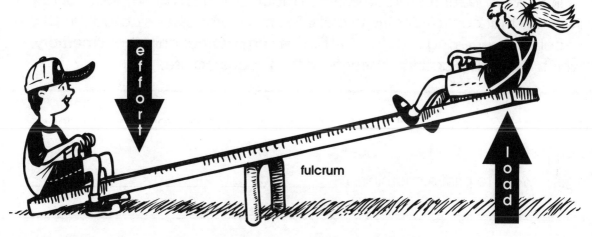

fulcrum

The force of **effort** lifts the **load** (the **resistance**) at the other end.

Draw a picture of a simple machine. Show how you could use a **lever** to pry a heavy rock out of the ground. Write captions using the vocabulary words.

# Make Connections

Read the paragraph. Think about the meaning of each **bold** word. Then, check the Student Dictionary.

> Click on an **icon** on the computer desktop, and a program opens. Pull down a **menu** and choose an action you want the program to perform. As you take these steps, the computer's **processors** are taking their own steps—at lightning speed! The processors are made of millions of tiny electronic switches that control electric circuits. The main processor is called the **CPU**, or central processing unit. The CPU is on a chip. Other chips hold **memory**, which is the **data** and the instructions the processors use.

Complete each sentence. Include the vocabulary word or words in your answer.

1. menu
   When I want to print something, I _____

   _____ .

2. processor, CPU
   A computer cannot really think like a person, but _____

   _____ .

3. icon
   If I want to open a program on my computer, I _____

   _____ .

4. memory, data
   I cannot play video games on this older computer because _____

   _____ .

 **Look It Up!**

Computer terms are similar to everyday words. Look up the words *menu* and *memory* in a classroom dictionary. Answer each question.

1. How is a computer menu like a restaurant menu? _____

   _____

2. How is a person's memory like a computer's memory? _____

   _____

# Play with Words

## Code Words

Choose the word or words that complete each sentence. Circle the letter.

1. Decomposed plants are a source of ___.
   c  geothermal energy
   d  a simple machine
   e  fossil fuel

2. A ___ encyclopedia has video clips.
   n  multimedia
   o  data
   p  mechanical

3. ___ is a force that slows motion.
   f  Electronic
   g  Friction
   h  Effort

4. An elbow joint is like ___.
   i  a fulcrum
   j  a load
   k  a force

5. A ___ is a simple machine.
   l  processor
   m  CPU
   n  lever

6. A small picture on a screen is ___.
   c  friction
   d  multimedia
   e  an icon

7. ___ keeps our feet on the ground.
   e  Gravity
   f  Effort
   g  A natural resource

8. Wind is a ___ source of energy.
   q  nonrenewable
   r  renewable
   s  gravity

Write the circled letters in order. You will find the name of a worker who creates technology.

_____

# Play with Words

## Synonym Mix-Up

Unscramble the letters to write a synonym for each vocabulary word.

1.  load          h t e w i g          _____

2.  solar energy   g i t n u s h l       _____

3.  nonrenewable   o n g e              _____

4.  menu           s t i l              _____

5.  fulcrum        t i v o p            _____

6.  effort         k r o w              _____

7.  icon           g e i m a            _____

8.  renewable      b l a p c a l r e e e  _____

## Technology Crossword Puzzle

Use the clues to complete the crossword puzzle.

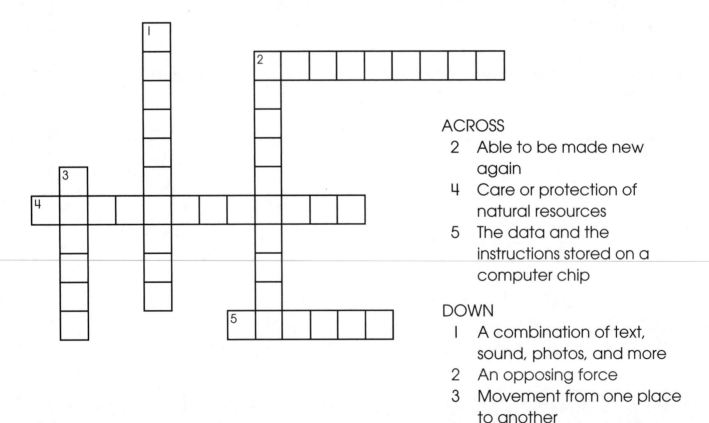

ACROSS
  2   Able to be made new again
  4   Care or protection of natural resources
  5   The data and the instructions stored on a computer chip

DOWN
  1   A combination of text, sound, photos, and more
  2   An opposing force
  3   Movement from one place to another

# Important Language Arts Words You Need to Know

Use this list to keep track of how well you know the new words.

0 = Don't Know          1 = Know It Somewhat          2 = Know It Well

___ adjective

___ adverb

___ agreement

___ antonym

___ apostrophe

___ author's purpose

___ character

___ compare and contrast

___ draft

___ essay

___ idiom

___ metaphor

___ mystery

___ opposite

___ outline

___ persuade

___ plot

___ plural

___ possession

___ prefix

___ pronoun

___ punctuation

___ research

___ root word

___ setting

___ similar

___ simile

___ singular

___ subject

___ suffix

___ summarize

___ suspense

___ synonym

___ topic sentence

# Explore a Word

Read the paragraph. Think about the meaning of the **bold** term.

> The pictures in the book help readers **compare and contrast** frogs and toads. These animals are alike in some ways and different in others.

1.  What do you think the term means? Write your idea.

    **compare and contrast:** _____

    _____

2.  Write a sentence with the term **compare and contrast**. Show what it means.

    _____

    _____

3.  Check the meaning of **compare and contrast** in the Student Dictionary.

4.  If your sentence in question 2 matches the meaning, put a ✓ after it. If your sentence does not match the meaning, write a better sentence.

    _____

    _____

5.  Make a simple drawing to show the meaning of **compare and contrast**.

Academic Vocabulary Practice • Grade 4 • CD-104809

# Explore a Word

Read the sentence. Think about the meaning of the **bold** word. Then, check the Student Dictionary.

The students did **research** to find information about their city's history.

Complete the web to show your understanding of the word *research*.

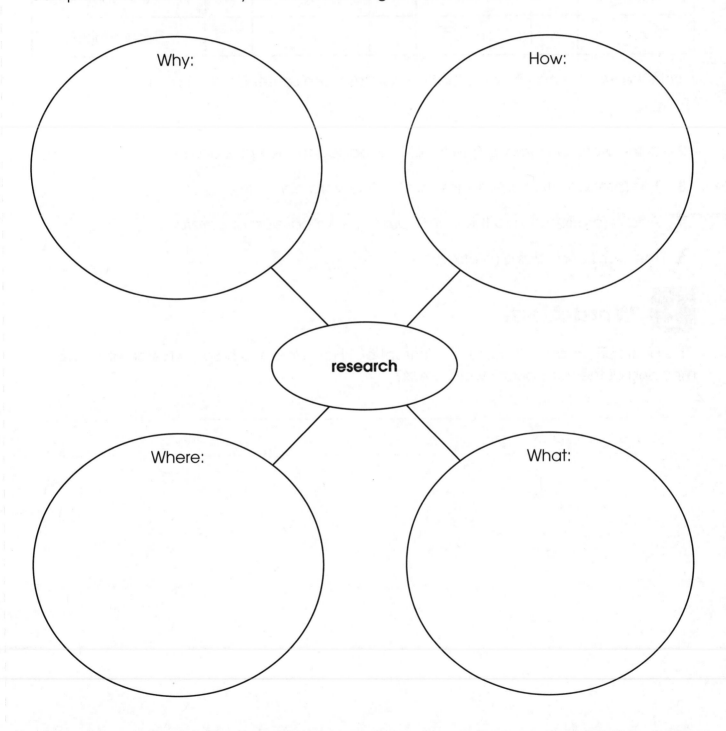

Why:

How:

research

Where:

What:

# Compare Words

Look at the word equations. Think about the meaning of each **bold** word. Then, check the Student Dictionary.

| Prefix | + | Word | + | Suffix | = | New Word |
|--------|---|------|---|--------|---|----------|
| re- | + | view | + | -er | = | reviewer |
| un- | + | clear | + | -ly | = | unclearly |
| dis- | + | agree | + | -able | = | disagreeable |

Circle the word in parentheses that completes each sentence.

1. In the word *agreement,* a (prefix/suffix) is added to the word *agree.*

2. In the word *disagree,* a (prefix/suffix) is added to the word *agree.*

3. The (prefix/suffix) *non-* means "not" in the word *nonsense.*

4. Add a (prefix/suffix) to the word *care* to make *careless* or *careful.*

5. The word *undo* has a (prefix/suffix).

 **Word Alert!**

The prefix *pre-* means "before" or "in front of." How does this help you remember the meaning of the vocabulary word *prefix*?

_____

_____

# Compare Words

Read the sentences and the examples. Think about the meaning of each **bold** word. Then, check the Student Dictionary.

A **synonym** is a word that has a **similar** meaning as another word.

Example: *smiles*

Nina *grins* at her cat.

An **antonym** is a word that has an **opposite** meaning of another word.

Example: *smiles*

Nina *frowns* at her cat.

Read each sentence. For each underlined word, write a synonym and an antonym.

|  | Synonym | Antonym |
|---|---|---|
| 1. He ate his dinner <u>quickly</u>. | _____ | _____ |
| 2. My cereal is <u>soggy</u>. | _____ | _____ |
| 3. My grandmother <u>laughs</u> a lot. | _____ | _____ |
| 4. The pilot was very <u>brave</u>. | _____ | _____ |
| 5. Tia's pet mouse was quite <u>ordinary</u>. | _____ | _____ |
| 6. She <u>broke</u> the window. | _____ | _____ |

 **Challenge!**

Write one interesting sentence using a synonym for *scream* and an antonym for *hold*.

_____

_____

# Compare Words

Read the advice column. Think about the meaning of each **bold** word. Then, check the Student Dictionary.

Dear Student Writer:

Make your writing interesting and clear by using sharp describing words. An **adjective** describes a person, a place, or a thing. You could use the adjective *good* to describe food. *The restaurant serves good food.* But, what are some better, sharper adjectives to use instead? How about using *spicy, fresh,* or *healthful*?

An **adverb** is another describing word. It describes how something is done. In these sentences, the adverbs are composed of a **root word** and the suffix *–ly*. *We looked at the menu hungrily. We ordered quickly. We ate happily.* Remember to use adverbs wisely!

Sincerely,

Helpful Hinter

Follow each instruction.

1. Write three adjectives to describe today's weather.

   _____

2. Write two adverbs to tell how someone spoke.

   _____

3. Write two adjectives to describe the noun *tree*.

   _____

4. What is the root of the word *unteachable*? *disenchanted*?

   _____

5. Rewrite the sentence. Add one adjective and one adverb to make it more interesting.

   The boys ate the pizza.

   _____

# Make Connections

Read the sentences and the examples. Think about the meaning of each **bold** word. Then, check the Student Dictionary.

A verb must agree with its **subject**. Check for subject-verb **agreement** in your sentences.

If the subject is a **singular** noun or the **pronoun** *he, she,* or *it,* add *–s* to the verb.

    Example: Jack <u>helps</u> his mother. She <u>depends</u> on him.
            subject  verb          subject  verb

If the subject is a **plural** noun or the pronoun *I, we, you,* or *they,* do not add *-s* to the verb.

    Example: The friends <u>meet</u> at the park. They <u>play</u> every day.
            subject   verb          subject verb

Find the five errors in this paragraph. Fix each error. Add notes to the writer, explaining why the sentences need to be fixed. Use the vocabulary words in your notes.

| | |
|---|---|
| ○ | My favorite color is green. It remind me of a forest of beautiful trees. Fresh green vegetables tastes great! |
| | A green, grassy lawn look like a welcome mat. I always wear something green. My parents drive a green car. We |
| ○ | lives in a green house on Green Street. Green things just makes me smile! |

# Make Connections

Read the sentences and the examples. Think about the meaning of each **bold** word. Then, check the Student Dictionary.

| A **simile** uses *like* or *as* to compare unlike things.  _____  Example: Felipe can be <u>as stubborn as a bulldog</u>! | A **metaphor** compares unlike things directly.  _____  Example: When Felipe wants something, <u>he is a bulldog</u>! | An **idiom** is a saying in which the words do not have their usual meaning.  _____  Example: Someday, Felipe will <u>learn his lesson</u>! |

Read each sentence. Underline the words that are a simile, a metaphor, or an idiom. Then, circle the correct description.

| | | | |
|---|---|---|---|
| 1. | Grace ran as fast as the wind. | simile | metaphor | idiom |
| 2. | The clouds are cotton balls. | simile | metaphor | idiom |
| 3. | She spoke in a voice like thunder! | simile | metaphor | idiom |
| 4. | Your answer is right on the button. | simile | metaphor | idiom |
| 5. | The playroom is a trash dump. | simile | metaphor | idiom |
| 6. | It is raining cats and dogs! | simile | metaphor | idiom |

 **Challenge!**

Choose one of the sentences above. Write another sentence that could come after it, telling more about the idea. Include a simile, a metaphor, or an idiom in your sentence.

_____

_____

_____

# Make Connections

Read the information. Think about the meaning of each **bold** word. Then, check the Student Dictionary.

One mark of **punctuation** is called the **apostrophe**. Below are three rules for using an apostrophe with the letter *s* to show **possession**.

| If the owner is a singular noun, use an apostrophe before the *s*. | If the owner is a plural noun, use an apostrophe after the *s*. | If the owner is an **irregular plural**, use the apostrophe before the *s*. |
|---|---|---|
| Examples: Emma's house, one boy's shirts | Examples: the girls' team, the friends' families | Examples: the children's room, the men's hats |

Follow each instruction.

1. Write a sentence with two punctuation marks.

   _____

   _____

2. Write a sentence about a girl with two pets. Use an apostrophe to show possession.

   _____

   _____

3. Write the irregular plurals of the words *mouse* and *woman*.

   _____

   _____

4. Write a sentence about the classrooms of three teachers. Use an apostrophe to show possession.

   _____

   _____

# Make Connections

Read the paragraph. Think about the meaning of each **bold** term. Then, check the Student Dictionary.

> Write an **essay** to **persuade** your readers to agree with you. Before you begin writing, make an **outline** as part of your planning. As you **draft**, write a **topic sentence** for each paragraph. For this essay, this will be your **author's purpose**.

Underline the correct ending to each sentence.

1. A common way people try to persuade others is
    A.   with advertising.
    B.   by storytelling.

2. The purpose of a topic sentence is
    A.   to prepare readers for a main idea.
    B.   to plan what you will include in your writing.

3. An outline is like a list of
    A.   books and other sources.
    B.   the ideas in a written work.

4. An essay is a kind of written work that
    A.   has a story problem, a setting, and characters.
    B.   shows the writer's knowledge and opinions.

5. After you write your first draft,
    A.   your essay is ready to hand in.
    B.   you usually revise your essay.

6. The author's purpose in writing a book titled *Anyone Can Grow a Garden* is probably
    A.   to show how many different kinds of flowers you can grow.
    B.   to show how easy gardening can be.

# Make Connections

Read the paragraph. Think about the meaning of each **bold** word. Then, check the Student Dictionary.

> If you like reading **mystery** stories filled with **suspense**, then I recommend reading *The Night Noises*. The **setting** of this story is an enchanted forest. The **plot** begins when the main **character** discovers a buried treasure in the woods. I would **summarize** the rest of the story, but I do not want to give away the ending!

Circle *Yes* or *No* for each question. Write your reason on the line.

1.  When you summarize, do you sum up what happened?          Yes          No

   _____

2.  Is the plot the same as the setting?          Yes          No

   _____

3.  Is suspense exciting?          Yes          No

   _____

4.  Is a mystery like a crime story?          Yes          No

   _____

5.  Is it possible to summarize a plot?          Yes          No

   _____

6.  Is there always just one character in a mystery?          Yes          No

   _____

# Look It Up!

Suspense can make you feel as if you are hanging in midair. Use a classroom dictionary to find the meaning of a related word, *suspend*. Explain how the meanings of *suspense* and *suspend* are related.

_____

_____

# Play with Words

## Code Words

Choose the word or words that complete each sentence. Circle the letter.

1. The word *happy* is an ___.
   r   adverb
   s   adjective
   t   essay

2. A ___ begins with a problem.
   e   plot
   f   simile
   g   plural

3. The word *child* has an ___.
   l   apostrophe
   m   idiom
   n   irregular plural

4. An apostrophe signals ___.
   t   possession
   u   pronouns
   v   agreement

5. *Befriend* and *friendly* have the same ___.
   c   mystery
   d   author's purpose
   e   root word

6. Introduce a paragraph with a ___.
   p   draft
   n   topic sentence
   r   character

7. A subject must be ___ with its verb.
   h   in suspense
   i   in outline
   c   in agreement

8. Can you ___ a metaphor and a simile?
   d   research and persuade
   e   compare and contrast
   f   outline and summarize

Write the circled letters in order. You will find a place to use punctuation.

in a _____

# Play with Words

## Letter by Letter

Choose the word that fits with each clue. Write it letter by letter. Some letters will be inside circles.

| antonym | character | essay | metaphor | outline |
|---------|-----------|-------|----------|---------|
| pronoun | setting | singular | suffix | |

1. *-ness*            _ Ⓞ _ _ _ _ _

2. *I, me, he, them*     _ _ _ Ⓞ _ _ _

3. A person in a story    _ _ _ _ Ⓞ _ _ _ _

4. Meaning just one      _ _ _ _ _ Ⓞ _ _

5. Where a story takes place   _ _ _ Ⓞ _ _ _

6. A word of pposite meaning   _ Ⓞ _ _ _ _ _

7. The phrase "A book is a treasure."   _ _ _ _ _ _ _ _ Ⓞ

8. A list of topics, subtopics, and details   _ _ _ _ Ⓞ _ _

9. A writing on a topic    _ _ _ _ Ⓞ

Write the circled letters in order. You will find the answer to this question: *What word do students always pronounce unclearly?*

_ _ _ _ _ _ _ _ _

# Important Social Studies Words You Need to Know

Use this list to keep track of how well you know the new words.

0 = Don't Know      1 = Know It Somewhat      2 = Know It Well

___ agreement

___ agriculture

___ ally

___ ancestor

___ artifact

___ bibliography

___ colonist

___ compromise

___ conflict

___ debate

___ diplomacy

___ diplomat

___ equality

___ evaluate

___ facts

___ found

___ frontier

___ game

___ generation

___ hardship

___ heritage

___ hunter-gatherers

___ independence

___ inhabitant

___ integration

___ international

___ irrigation

___ liberty

___ Loyalist

___ majority

___ migration

___ militia

___ national

___ nomadic

___ Patriot

___ pioneer

___ population

___ primary source

___ protest

___ reliable

___ research

___ secondary source

___ segregation

___ territory

___ tradition

___ treaty

___ unreliable

___ works cited

# Explore a Word

Read the sentence. Think about the meaning of the **bold** word.

> The American colonies fought a war for **independence** from Britain.

1. What do you think the word means? Write your idea.

   **independence:** _____

   _____

2. Write a sentence with the word **independence**. Show what it means.

   _____

   _____

3. Check the meaning of **independence** in the Student Dictionary.

4. If your sentence in question 3 matches the meaning, put a ✓ after it. If your sentence does not match the meaning, write a better sentence.

   _____

   _____

5. Make a simple drawing to show the meaning of **independence**.

# Explore a Word

Read the sentences. Think about the meaning of each **bold** word. Then, check the Student Dictionary.

> If nations cannot settle their differences peacefully, the result is **conflict**.
>
> Travelers faced many **hardships** as they crossed the desert. Lack of water was one of the big problems.

Complete the charts to show your understanding of the words *conflict* and *hardship*.

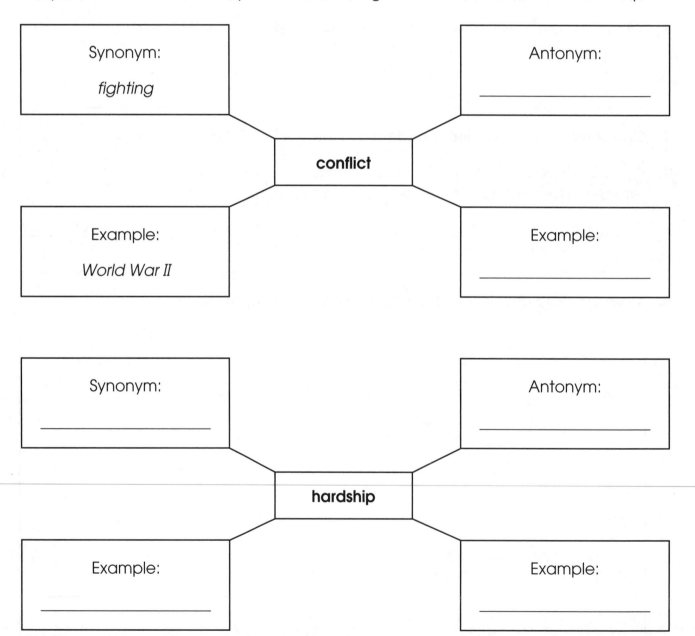

Synonym:

*fighting*

Antonym:

_____

**conflict**

Example:

*World War II*

Example:

_____

Synonym:

_____

Antonym:

_____

**hardship**

Example:

_____

Example:

_____

# Compare Words

Read the paragraph. Think about the meaning of each **bold** word. Then, check the Student Dictionary.

> The **national** news report told about Louisiana and Texas. The **international** news report told about China and Japan.

Circle the word in parentheses that completes each sentence.

1. Trucks drive from Florida to California on (national/international) highways.

2. Trade among countries is (national/international).

3. America's (national/international) anthem is "The Star-Spangled Banner."

4. (National/International) laws protect the world's oceans.

5. Athletes from many countries compete in (national/international) games.

 ## Word Alert!

A prefix is a word part added before a word. A suffix is a word part added to the end of a word. Prefixes and suffixes change word meanings.

| Prefix | Word | Suffix | Meaning |
|---|---|---|---|
| *inter-* means "between" | *nation* | *-al* makes a describing word | *international* means "involving two or more nations" |

6. Make another word using the prefix and suffix above.

   _____

7. Can you write a sentence with the longer word?

   _____

   _____

   _____

# Compare Words

Look at the pictures and read the captions. Think about the meaning of each **bold** term. Then, check the Student Dictionary.

primary source        secondary source

Read the questions. Use your answers to fill in the chart. Then, add more details to the chart.

- What can you learn from both kinds of sources?
- When are secondary sources written?
- Why do historians study primary sources?
- What kind of source is a president's speech? a history textbook? an encyclopedia? an eyewitness account?

| Primary Source | Both | Secondary Source |
|---|---|---|
|  |  |  |
|  |  |  |

# Make Connections

Read the paragraphs. Think about the meaning of each **bold** word. Then, check the Student Dictionary.

> Nonfiction writing is based on **facts** or real events. Nonfiction writers must **research** their topics. They read, watch, or listen to sources to gather information. They **evaluate** the accuracy and **reliability** of their sources before writing. The facts they use must be correct. If a source is inaccurate, the writer will not use it. If a source is **unreliable** and the writer does not trust it, he will not use it.
>
> A nonfiction writer must keep track of his sources. He may add a **bibliography** or a **works cited** page to the end of his work.

Complete each sentence. Include the vocabulary word or phrase in your answer.

1. works cited
   If I want to know where the writer found the information on tigers, _____

   _____ .

2. reliable
   I spoke to someone who was actually at the parade, _____

   _____ .

3. evaluate
   The two sources did not agree on when the battle took place, _____

   _____ .

4. research
   I do not know anything about gorillas, _____

   _____ .

5. facts
   I am writing a fiction story about dragons, _____

   _____ .

6. bibliography
   I would like to learn even more about Japan, _____

   _____ .

# Make Connections

Read the paragraph. Think about the meaning of each **bold** word. Then, check the Student Dictionary.

> Britain ruled the American colonies. Some **colonists** were **Loyalists** and felt strong ties to Britain. But, the **majority** of colonists wanted **liberty** from the British king's laws. They created their own **militia** to combat the British troops. These colonists dreamed of a separate American nation. They were known as **Patriots**.

Circle the word in parentheses that completes each sentence.

1. American colonists who fought against Britain were called (Patriots/Loyalists).

2. American colonists who sided with Britain were (Patriots/Loyalists).

3. The (Patriots/Loyalists) wanted to obey Britain's laws.

4. The (Patriots/Loyalists) wanted liberty and independence for the colonies.

5. The (Patriots/Loyalists) won the American Revolution.

6. The (Patriots/Loyalist) formed local militias to fight the British troops.

 **Word Alert!**

Words that belong to the same word family have related meanings. Complete the sentences with words from the word bank.

| | | |
|---|---|---|
| patriot | patriotism | loyalty |
| patriotic | loyal | loyally |

1. A _____ loves his or her country. Saluting the flag is a sign of _____. Defending one's country is a _____ act.

2. People can be _____ to a leader. They show their _____ by giving steady support. They speak and act _____.

# Make Connections

Read the paragraph. Think about the meaning of each **bold** term. Then, check the Student Dictionary.

> Early people lived as **hunter-gatherers**. They ate roots, seeds, and other wild plants that they gathered. They hunted **game** for food. Many groups were **nomadic** and followed the animals they hunted. This way of life changed when **agriculture** began and people started to grow crops. **Irrigation** practices improved, bringing essential water to crops, and farming settlements grew.

Circle *Yes* or *No* for each question. Write your reason on the line.

1. Do nomadic people build large cities?                                 Yes     No

   _____

2. Are most hunter-gatherers also farmers?                               Yes     No

   _____

3. Is agriculture the same as farming?                                   Yes     No

   _____

4. Is corn an example of game?                                           Yes     No

   _____

5. Are hunter-gatherers nomadic?                                         Yes     No

   _____

6. Is irrigation necessary to a nomadic way of life?                     Yes     No

   _____

 **Look It Up!**

Each meaning of a word is numbered in a dictionary entry. Look up the word *game* in a classroom dictionary. Write the meaning that fits with this page.

_____

# Make Connections

Read the paragraph. Think about the meaning of each **bold** word. Then, check the Student Dictionary.

> **Diplomats** from both nations worked together to try to avoid a conflict over land. It seems as if an **agreement** would never be reached. Finally, the diplomats made key **compromises**. Their **diplomacy** was successful. The leaders of both countries signed a **treaty** that was considered fair by everyone involved. Instead of becoming enemies, the two nations were now **allies**.

Underline the correct ending to each sentence.

1. If you use diplomacy,
    A. you probably will not hurt anyone's feelings.
    B. you probably will make enemies.

2. If you get along well with everyone,
    A. you might make a good ally.
    B. you might make a good diplomat.

3. The war ended
    A. when all nations signed a peace treaty.
    B. when both sides refused to compromise.

4. If you are a diplomatic person,
    A. you try to create conflict.
    B. you try to avoid conflict.

5. If you want to start a new school club,
    A. it is helpful to have an ally.
    B. it is helpful to sign a treaty.

 **Challenge!**

Think of a difficult situation at school where diplomacy might help. Explain.

_____

_____

_____

# Make Connections

| ancestor | artifacts | generation | heritage | traditions |

Check the Student Dictionary for the meaning of each vocabulary word in the word bank. Read each set of listed things. Think about why they belong together. Then, write the vocabulary word that names the category.

1. _____

    festive meals
    stories from long ago
    decorative clothing

2. _____

    a group of cousins
    a period of about 30 years
    parents, uncles, and aunts

3. _____

    A grandmother's grandfather
    a relative from long ago
    a great-great-great-grandparent

4. _____

    stone arrowheads found in a cave
    broken pottery buried in the sand
    polished pieces of bone frozen in a glacier

5. _____

    something passed down through time
    beliefs shared with people who came before you
    a connection with the past

## ⭐ Challenge!

Write one interesting sentence using three of the vocabulary words.

_____

_____

# Make Connections

| debate | equality | integration | protest | segregation |

Check the Student Dictionary for the meaning of each vocabulary word in the word bank. Read the paragraphs. Write the vocabulary words that could replace the **bold** words.

1.  Until the 1950s, African American children in southern states could not go to schools with white children. State laws required the **separation** of people based on race.

    _____

2.  African Americans did not have the same chance for education that white people had. They did not have the same chance for jobs. Leaders stepped forward to fight for **balanced chances** for all people.

    _____

3.  One of the leaders was Martin Luther King Jr. He believed that people should **object to** unfair laws in peaceful ways.

    _____

4.  Martin Luther King Jr. helped organize marches. Thousands of people marched to support the **opening to all people** of public schools, buildings, and other places.

    _____

5.  The **argument** about civil rights is an important part of American history.

    _____

 ## Challenge!

Write one sentence using the words *integration* and *segregation*.

_____

_____

Academic Vocabulary Practice • Grade 4 • CD-104809

# Make Connections

Read the paragraph. Think about the meaning of each **bold** word. Then, check the Student Dictionary.

> The **frontier** of the United States kept moving westward. **Pioneers** cleared forests, built cabins, and began farming. They **founded** new communities. As **migration** west continued, the **population** in the new **territories** grew. Areas with just a few **inhabitants** grew into thriving towns.

Circle *Yes* or *No* for each question. Write your reason on the line.

1. A group wanted to found a settlement. Had they lost it?     Yes     No

_____

2. Is a frontier a kind of place?     Yes     No

_____

3. Does an inhabitant usually live in a wild land?     Yes     No

_____

4. Is a pioneer like an explorer?     Yes     No

_____

5. Could pioneers be inhabitants?     Yes     No

_____

6. Does migration usually occur between neighborhoods?     Yes     No

_____

 # Look It Up!

Some words that look alike come from different origins. These words have separately numbered entries in a dictionary. Look up the word *found* in a classroom dictionary. Write the meaning that fits with each word.

1. The city was founded in 1700.

_____

2. Have you found the city on the map?

_____

Name _____

# Play with Words

## Letter by Letter

Choose the word that fits with each clue. Write it letter by letter. Some letters will be inside circles.

| ancestor | conflict | heritage | liberty | majority |
| militia | nomad | protest | segregation | treaty |

1. This is a person who wanders. — — — — ◯

2. This kept groups apart. — — — — — — — — ◯ — —

3. Grandfather's grandmother — — ◯ — — — — —

4. This is not a regular army. — — — — ◯ — —

5. This comes from the past. — — — ◯ — — — —

6. This is a way to say no. — — ◯ — — — —

7. War is one example. — — ◯ — — — — —

8. This is an agreement. — — — — — ◯ —

9. This is more than half. — — — — ◯ — — — —

10. This is freedom. — — — — — — ◯

Write the circled letters in order. You will find the answer to this question: *Where does Friday come before Thursday?*

in a __ __ __ __ __ __ __ __ __ __ __

# Play with Words

## Synonym Pairs

Read each clue. Find and circle the two synonyms that match the clue.

|   |   |   |
|---|---|---|
| 1. | Sign this to make a promise. | i f t r e a t y a j a g r e e m e n t o b i s |
| 2. | Without this, we do not eat. | w o f a r m i n g r t h a g r i c u l t u r e d o |
| 3. | This is a loyal friend. | i n p a r t n e r g i a l l y |
| 4. | Make your views known with this. | t s d e b a t e w o a r g u m e n t r t h |
| 5. | This person goes first. | d o s c o u t i n p i o n e e r g w |
| 6. | This is passed down through time. | e l l t r a d i t i o n a t h e r i t a g e r a |
| 7. | Everyone wants to be treated with this. | d i t e q u a l i t y i o n f a i r n e s s a l |
| 8. | This is movement to a new place. | s a m i g r a t i o n y i j o u r n e y n g |

Look back to find the letters you did NOT circle. Write them in order to find a message.

__ __  __  __ __ __  __ __  __ __ __ __ __

__ __ __ __ __,  __ __ ' __  __ __ __ __ __

__ __ __ __ __  __ __ __ __ __!

( __  __ __ __ __ __ __ __ __ __ __ __ __  __ __ __ __ __ __ __ )

# Play with Words

## Synonym Mix-Up

Unscramble the letters to write a synonym for each vocabulary word.

1. independence     r d e f e m o     _____

2. territory     r g o i e n     _____

3. found     r c a e t e     _____

4. international     b l g o a l     _____

5. conflict     t t b l a e     _____

6. tradition     s t u m o c     _____

7. debate     c u d i s s s     _____

8. nomadic     m o a r i n g     _____

## Social Studies Crossword Puzzle

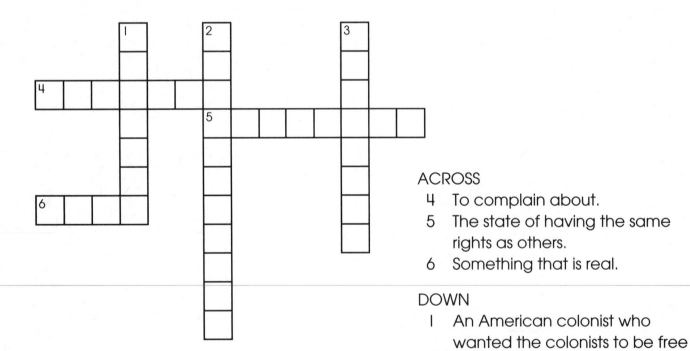

ACROSS
4  To complain about.
5  The state of having the same rights as others.
6  Something that is real.

DOWN
1  An American colonist who wanted the colonists to be free of British rule.
2  Making schools, parks, buses, or other public places open to people of all races.
3  Dependable.

# Play with Words

## Code Words

Choose the word or words that completes each sentence. Circle the letter.

1. Newcomers settled in the ___.
   - **g** hardship
   - **h** territory
   - **i** inhabitant

2. ___ traveled west in wagon trains.
   - **i** Pioneers
   - **j** Patriots
   - **k** Loyalists

3. Was the nation an enemy or an ___?
   - **q** international
   - **r** evaluate
   - **s** ally

4. Keep track of your sources in ___.
   - **t** a bibliography
   - **u** a compromise
   - **v** an essay

5. In dry areas, crops need ___.
   - **n** agriculture
   - **o** irrigation
   - **p** hunter-gatherers

6. Cousins belong to the same ___.
   - **p** primary sources
   - **q** research
   - **r** generation

7. Nomads were ___.
   - **h** works cited
   - **i** hunter-gatherers
   - **j** diplomats

8. Americans Indians were the first ___ of Ohio.
   - **a** Patriots
   - **b** frontier
   - **c** inhabitants

Write the circled letters in order. You will find a word that describes an important event.

_____

# Important Geography
# Words You Need to Know

Use this list to keep track of how well you know the new words.

0 = Don't Know          1 = Know It Somewhat          2 = Know It Well

___ adapt                          ___ tropics

___ Antarctic                      ___ tundra

___ Arctic                         ___ wetlands

___ biome

___ canyon

___ cardinal direction

___ compass rose

___ conservation

___ degree

___ delta

___ equator

___ floodplain

___ glacier

___ globe

___ hemisphere

___ latitude

___ longitude

___ plateau

___ prime meridian

___ region

___ strait

___ swamp

# Explore a Word

Read the paragraph. Think about the meaning of the **bold** word.

> Some of the natural **regions** on Earth include rain forests, deserts, and grasslands. A region can be made of people, too. Groups in the same cultural region usually speak the same language and share the same ways of life.

1. What do you think the word means? Write your idea.

   **region:** _____

   _____

2. Write a sentence with the word **region**. Show what it means.

   _____

   _____

3. Check the meaning of **region** in the Student Dictionary.

4. If your sentence in question 2 matches the meaning, put a ✓ after it. If your sentence does not match the meaning, write a better sentence.

   _____

   _____

5. Make a simple drawing to show the meaning of **region**.

# Compare Words

Look at the picture and read the captions. Think about the meaning of each **bold** word. Then, check the Student Dictionary.

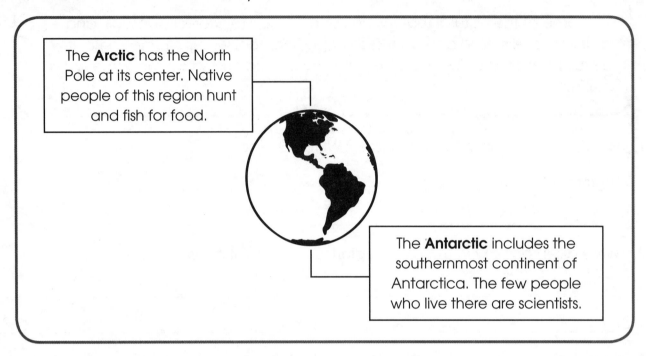

The **Arctic** has the North Pole at its center. Native people of this region hunt and fish for food.

The **Antarctic** includes the southernmost continent of Antarctica. The few people who live there are scientists.

Circle the word in parentheses that completes each sentence.

1. The (Arctic, Antarctic) includes the South Pole.

2. The Inuit are native people of the (Arctic, Antarctic).

3. Penguins of the southern oceans come ashore in the (Arctic, Antarctic).

4. Summer at the North Pole is winter in the (Arctic, Antarctic).

5. The northern parts of Canada are in the (Arctic, Antarctic).

 **Look It Up!**

The word *Arctic* can be an adjective that describes a noun. For example, *Arctic region*, *Arctic mammals*, and *Arctic people*. The word *arctic*, spelled with a lowercase *a*, is also an adjective. Look up *arctic* in a classroom dictionary. Use it to describe three nouns.

_____

_____

_____

# Compare Words

Look at the picture and read the caption. Think about the meaning of each **bold** word. Then, check the Student Dictionary.

The **equator** is an imaginary line that cuts Earth in half. One **hemisphere** is north of the equator, and the other is south of it.

Circle *Yes* or *No* for each question. Write your reason on the line.

1. Is the Arctic in the Southern Hemisphere?                Yes     No

_____

2. Is a hemisphere half of the globe?                       Yes     No

_____

3. Is it possible to step across the equator?               Yes     No

_____

4. Does the equator cross Antarctica?                       Yes     No

_____

5. Could a country be in two hemispheres?                   Yes     No

_____

6. Is the United States north of the equator?               Yes     No

_____

# Compare Words

Look at the pictures and read the caption. Think about the meaning of each **bold** word. Then, check the Student Dictionary.

Global Projection Map

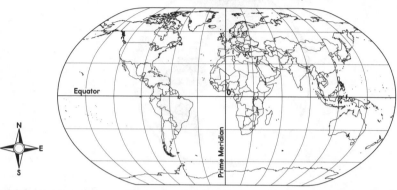

A **globe** is a spherical model of Earth. To read a globe, you must know the four **cardinal directions**: north, south, east, and west. The two most important lines on a globe are the equator and the **prime meridian**. The prime meridian is an imaginary line that cuts Earth in half vertically. The Western Hemisphere is west of the prime meridian, and the Eastern Hemisphere is east of it.

Complete each sentence. Include the vocabulary word or phrase in your answer.

1. cardinal direction
   The direction northeast _____

   _____ .

2. Western Hemisphere
   The continent of Asia is _____

   _____ .

3. prime meridian
   The imaginary line that runs from _____

   _____ .

4. Eastern Hemisphere
   The prime meridian divides _____

   _____ .

# Make Connections

Look at the map and read the caption. Think about the meaning of each **bold** term. Then, check the Student Dictionary.

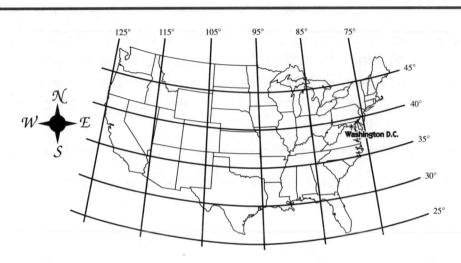

Lines of **latitude** go east–west. Lines of **longitude** go north–south. A **compass rose** shows direction. Because Earth is a sphere, we measure latitude and longitude in **degrees**.

Use the vocabulary words to complete the paragraphs. Use each word twice.

Where in the world is your town? To find the answer, look on a map. The

(1.) _____ points north. Is your town in the eastern or western part of your

state? The (2.) _____ will help you find those directions.

Where, exactly, is the capital of the United States? Maps have lines that help you

find locations. (3.) _____ is measured in (4.) _____ north or

south of the equator. (5.) _____ is measured in (6.) _____

east or west of the prime meridian, which runs north–south through Greenwich

(pronounced *GREH-nich*), England. Washington, DC, has a (7.) _____

of 38° north. Its (8.) _____ is 77° west.

# Make Connections

Read the paragraph. Think about the meaning of each **bold** word. Then, check the Student Dictionary.

> We began our trip by riding a ferry across the **strait**. Then, we took a bus to view a giant **glacier**. We walked across its icy surface! After that, we rode on a train across a **plateau**. When the flat land ended, the train dipped down. At last, we drove to a **canyon**. We peered down its steep walls.

Complete each sentence. Include the vocabulary word in your answer.

1. glaciers
   The Great Lakes formed during the last ice age when _____

   _____ .

2. physical features
   Maps show rivers, mountains, _____

   _____ .

3. canyon
   A valley is a low area of land, but _____

   _____ .

4. plateau
   A hill often has a round top, but _____

   _____ .

5. strait
   Ships sailing from the lake to the bay must _____

   _____ .

# Make Connections

Read the paragraph. Think about the meaning of each **bold** word. Then, check the Student Dictionary.

> People have **adapted** to every **biome** in the world. They have learned to live in the freezing **tundra**, the humid **tropics**, and the driest deserts. The world's human population is higher now than ever before.

Underline the correct ending to each sentence.

1.  People of the tundra depended on animals for food because
    A.  the soil did not support crops.
    B.  animals were easy to find.

2.  A biome covers a large area in which
    A.  there are similar kinds of plants and animals.
    B.  the weather conditions are harsh.

3.  Lands in the tropics generally have
    A.  long winters and short summers.
    B.  warm or hot temperatures all year.

4.  The population of a region always
    A.  grows larger.
    B.  changes over time.

5.  People have learned to adapt to
    A.  lands with different climates and vegetation.
    B.  homes, clothing, and methods of finding food.

 **Word Alert!**

Words that belong to the same word family have related meanings. Write a sentence that contains the three words from the word bank.

> adapted        adaptable        adaptation

_____

_____

# Make Connections

Read the paragraph. Think about the meaning of each **bold** word. Then, check the Student Dictionary.

> The **conservation** of **wetlands** is important. For example, a **swamp** helps filter water and refill underground water supplies. Swamps often develop in the **floodplains** of a river. The river creates valuable wetlands in its **delta** as it empties into the sea.

Use your ideas to complete each sentence with a word or a phrase that makes sense.

1. People work on conservation projects to _____ land, water, and life.

2. A swamp is a home to trees that can _____ in water.

3. A delta often has rich soil that the river _____.

4. A floodplain is a land that stretches on both sides of _____.

5. A wetland is valuable because it helps protect _____.  .

 ## Word Alert!

Two words put together are called a *compound word*. Two of the vocabulary words are compound words. Write a meaning for each compound word. Include both of the smaller words in your meaning.

_____

_____

_____

_____

# Play with Words

## If So, Then Write

Read the instructions. Then, write the correct letter in the blank. When you finish, you should have spelled a geography word.

___ ___ ___ ___ ___ ___ ___ ___ ___ ___
 1   2   3   4   5   6   7   8   9   10

1.  If lines of latitude cross north and south, write *P* on blank 1. If lines of latitude cross east and west, write *C* on blank 1.

2.  If a hemisphere is exactly half of the globe, write *O* on blank 2. If a hemisphere is less than half of the globe, write *L* on blank 2.

3.  If glaciers are in the Arctic, write *N* on blank 3. If glaciers are not in the Arctic, write *T* on blank 3.

4.  If the prime meridian runs east–west, write *S* on blank 4. If the prime meridian runs north–south, write *T* on blank 4.

5.  If a population has to do with people, write *I* on blank 5. If a population has nothing to do with people, write *E* on blank 5.

6.  If biomes are measured in degrees, write *A* on blank 6. If lines of latitude are measured in degrees, write *N* on blank 6.

7.  If a strait is narrow, write *E* on blank 7. If a strait is wide, write *O* on blank 7.

8.  If a line of longitude crosses the Antarctic, write *N* on blank 8. If a line of longitude does not cross the Antarctic, write *M* on blank 8.

9.  If a compass rose is a physical feature, write *R* on blank 9. If a canyon is a physical feature, write *T* on blank 9.

10. If a tundra is a biome, write *S* on blank 10. If a tundra is a plateau, write *O* on blank 10.

# Play with Words

## Code Words

Choose the word or words that complete each sentence. Circle the letter.

1. A ___ is like a river of ice.
   l  delta
   m  glacier
   n  strait

2. A tropical rain forest is a ___.
   m  swamp
   n  globe
   o  biome

3. ___ lines are imaginary.
   u  Longitude
   v  Glacier
   w  Cardinal direction

4. The North Pole is in the ___.
   l  equator
   m  Antarctic
   n  Arctic

5. High, flat land is a ___.
   t  plateau
   u  canyon
   v  floodplain

6. Cities have high ___.
   a  population
   b  hemisphere
   c  conservation

7. A line of ___ runs north–south.
   h  latitude
   i  longitude
   j  equator

8. The ___ on a map points north.
   m  equator
   n  compass rose
   o  strait

Write the circled letters in order. You will find the name of a physical feature.

_____

Academic Vocabulary Practice • Grade 4 • CD-104809

# Play with Words

## Letter by Letter

Choose the word that fits with each clue. Write it letter by letter. Some letters will be inside circles.

> biome     conservation     delta     equator     floodplain
>
> hemisphere     swamp     tropics     tundra

1. Half of the globe    __ __ __ __ __ __ Ⓞ __ __

2. V-shaped land at a river's mouth    __ __ __ __ Ⓞ

3. Protection    __ __ __ __ __ __ __ Ⓞ __ __ __ __

4. Line at 0° latitude    Ⓞ __ __ __ __ __ __

5. Florida's Everglades    __ __ __ __ Ⓞ

6. Where polar bears live    __ __ __ __ __ Ⓞ

7. Land along a river    __ __ __ __ __ __ __ Ⓞ __ __ __

8. An ecosystem    __ __ __ __ Ⓞ

9. Where rain forests grow    __ __ __ __ __ __ Ⓞ

Write the circled letters in order. You will find the answer to this riddle: *How are your hands like a tropical region?*

Both __ __ __ __ __    __ __ __ __ __ __ .

Academic Vocabulary Practice • Grade 4 • CD-104809

Name _____

# Important Civics and Economics Words You Need to Know

Use this list to keep track of how well you know the new words.

0 = Don't Know        1 = Know It Somewhat        2 = Know It Well

___ amendment

___ Articles of Confederation

___ Bill of Rights

___ branches of government

___ capital resources

___ Constitution

___ demand

___ elect

___ executive

___ House of Representatives

___ human resources

___ industry

___ judicial

___ jury

___ labor

___ legislative

___ natural resources

___ production

___ representation

___ scarcity

___ Senate

___ suffrage

___ supply

___ surplus

___ vote

Name _____

# Explore a Word

Read the paragraph. Think about the meaning of the **bold** word.

> The island nation had no mining **industry**, few factories, and a small fishing industry. Its main source of wealth was the tourism industry.

1. What do you think the word means? Write your idea.

   **industry:** _____

   _____

2. Write a sentence with the word **industry**. Show what it means.

   _____

   _____

3. Check the meaning of **industry** in the Student Dictionary.

4. If your sentence in question 2 matches the meaning, put a ✓ after it. If your sentence does not match the meaning, write a better sentence.

   _____

   _____

5. Make a simple drawing to show the meaning of **industry**.

# Compare Words

Read the paragraph. Think about the meaning of each **bold** word. Then, check the Student Dictionary.

> How much does something cost? The price depends on **supply** and **demand**. Supply is the amount of a product that sellers are willing and able to sell at various prices. The demand is the amount of the product that buyers are willing and able to buy at various prices. If there is a **surplus** of goods, there is more than enough to satisfy all of the buyers. If there is a **scarcity** of goods, there is not enough to go around to all of the buyers. When supply and demand are in balance, the price is right for both sellers and buyers.

Complete each sentence with your own ideas about supply, demand, and price.

1. The new gadgets are so popular that stores have run out of them. The supply _____

   _____

   _____ .

2. The market price for a cup of lemonade is about 50¢. Mason opened a lemonade stand and charged $10 for each cup. The demand for Mason's lemonade

   _____

   _____ .

3. It was a stormy season, and orange growers lost a lot of their crop. Oranges are now scarce. The price of oranges is high because the supply _____

   _____ .

4. Your favorite breakfast cereal just doubled in price! Demand may _____

   _____

   _____ .

5. There is a surplus of lawn mowers in the stores this year, _____

   _____ .

# Make Connections

Read the paragraph. Think about the meaning of each **bold** word. Then, check the Student Dictionary.

**Suffrage** is valuable. The right to **vote** gives citizens a say in how they are governed. In the United States, voters in each state have **representation** in two main ways. They **elect** two lawmakers to the **Senate**. They also elect lawmakers to the **House of Representatives**. The number of representatives depends on the state's population.

Underline the correct ending to each sentence.

1. In the United States, voters elect
    A.  the size of their state's population.
    B.  the people who will represent them in government.

2. US citizens have representation in
    A.  the Senate and the House of Representatives.
    B.  the House of Representatives.

3. Before women gained suffrage, they
    A.  could not vote.
    B.  had representation.

4. Suffrage has been granted to
    A.  all US citizens of voting age.
    B.  the whole population.

5. Representation matters to citizens because
    A.  only senators can vote.
    B.  they want lawmakers to serve them.

6. Everyone in both the Senate and the House of Representatives
    A.  must have been elected by people in their cities.
    B.  must have been elected by people in their states.

## Make Connections

Name _____

Read the paragraph. Think about the meaning of each **bold** term. Then, check the Student Dictionary.

> The **Articles of Confederation** was the original constitution of the 13 founding colonies. It was replaced by the **Constitution** of the United States in 1789. The Constitution has been slightly changed since then. The **Bill of Rights** is the name of the first 10 **amendments** to the Constitution. Amendments five through eight protect the rights of people accused of crimes. This includes the right to a speedy and public trial by a **jury**.

Complete each sentence with one or two words that make sense.

1. The founders of the United States wrote the Constitution to _____ a government.

2. The Constitution explains how to make amendments that will _____ the law of the land.

3. The Articles of Confederation was a set of laws used by people in the

   _____.

4. A jury is made up of citizens who are expected to _____.

5. The First Amendment protects basic freedoms such as the right to practice one's religion and the right to _____ in speech and print.

 **Look It Up!**

What is the difference between a constitution and the Constitution? Use a classroom dictionary to find the meaning of each word. Then, write a sentence to explain the difference.

_____

_____

Name _____

# Make Connections

Read the chart. Think about the meaning of each **bold** term. Then, check the Student Dictionary.

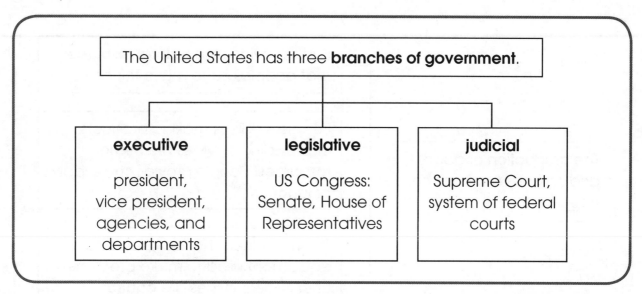

Use the vocabulary words to complete the paragraphs. Some words will be used twice.

The word *execute* can mean "to carry out" or "to put into action." The

(1.) _____ branch carries out laws, making sure that they are obeyed. The

laws are written by members of the (2.) _____ branch. Judgments about

the laws are made by the (3.) _____ branch.

Each of these (4.) _____ can limit the power

of the others. For example, the (5.) _____ branch appoints federal court

judges. But, the president's choices must be approved by lawmakers in the

(6.) _____ branch. The judges in the (7.) _____ branch, in turn,

can decide that actions taken by the president or Congress are not permitted by

the US Constitution.

# Make Connections

Look at the chart. Think about the meaning of each **bold** term. Then, check the Student Dictionary.

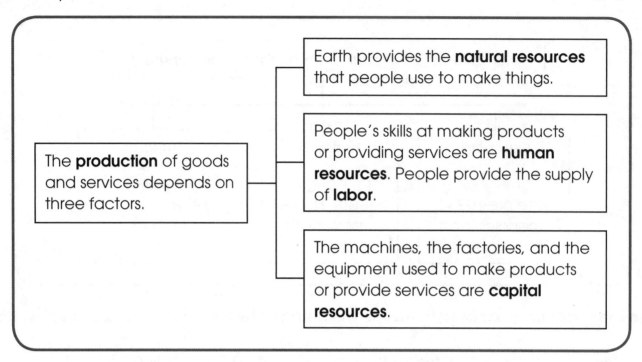

The **production** of goods and services depends on three factors.

Earth provides the **natural resources** that people use to make things.

People's skills at making products or providing services are **human resources**. People provide the supply of **labor**.

The machines, the factories, and the equipment used to make products or provide services are **capital resources**.

Circle *Yes* or *No* for each question. Write your reason on the line.

1. Is labor needed for production?                                          Yes     No

   _____

2. Is a carpenter's hammer an example of a natural resource?                 Yes     No

   _____

3. Would a dentist need capital resources to run an office?                  Yes     No

   _____

4. Are workers human resources?                                             Yes     No

   _____

5. Are natural resources made from capital resources?                        Yes     No

   _____

6. Is a T-shirt factory involved in the production of a service?             Yes     No

   _____

# Play with Words

## Code Words

Choose the word or words that complete each sentence. Circle the letter.

1. Skilled labor is a ___.
   q  branch of government
   r  natural resource
   s  human resource

2. Americans ___ lawmakers to the Senate.
   u  elect
   v  vote
   w  legislative

3. The ___ protects freedom of speech.
   e  human resource
   f  Bill of Rights
   g  legislative branch

4. The number of lawmakers in the US House of Representatives depends on a state's ___.
   d  industry
   e  surplus
   f  population

5. Voters want ___ in Congress.
   q  capital resources
   r  representation
   s  demand

6. ___ provides jobs.
   a  Industry
   b  Jury
   c  The Constitution

7. The US president is in the ___ branch.
   e  judicial
   f  legislative
   g  executive

8. The Thirteenth ___ ended slavery.
   c  jury
   d  Senate
   e  Amendment

Write the circled letters in order. You will find the name of something that is necessary in a democracy.

_____

# Play with Words

## Two or Three

Read each clue. Find and circle the two or three words that match the clue.

1.  Bill of Rights                                w h f i r s t a t e n t a m e n d m e n t s

2.  water, minerals, soil                       i n a t u r a l s a l r e s o u r c e s w a

3.  concerns of judges                        y s r i j u d i c i a l g h m a t t e r s t i

4.  the first constitution               n f r a r t i c l e s o o f n c o n f e d e r a t i o n t o f

5.  forces that act on prices            y o u s u p p l y y e a n d t y d e m a n d o u

6.  protection of voting rights         c a s u f f r a g e n n e v a m e n d m e n t e r

7.  too much supply or too much demand      s e s u r p l u s e o r i s c a r c i t y t y o

8.  US Constitution                         u r n a t i o n a l f u l a w t u r e

Look back to find the letters you did NOT circle. Write them in order to find a riddle and its answer.

____ ____ ____ ____   ____ ____   ____ ____ ____ ____ ____ ____

____ ____ ____ ____ ____   ____ ____

____ ____ ____ ____ ____   ____ ____   ____ ____ ____ ,   ____ ____ ____

____ ____ ____   ____ ____ ____ ____   ____ ____ ____ ____ ____   ____ ____ ____   ____ ____?

( ____ ____ ____ ____   ____ ____ ____ ____ ____ ____ )

# Important Art
# Words You Need to Know

Use this list to keep track of how well you know the new words.

0 = Don't Know          1 = Know It Somewhat          2 = Know It Well

___ background

___ brass

___ collage

___ conductor

___ cue

___ expression

___ gesture

___ improvise

___ mosaic

___ mural

___ orchestra

___ pastel

___ percussion

___ perspective

___ portrait

___ posture

___ profile

___ prop

___ rhythmical

___ script

___ set

___ shading

___ stencil

___ strings

___ three-dimensional

___ two-dimensional

___ watercolor

___ woodwinds

# Explore a Word

Read the paragraph. Think about the meaning of the **bold** word.

> Actors speak with **expression**. Musicians play with expression. A sculpture is an expression of the sculptor's idea. Art is an expression of feeling, experience, and more.

1. What do you think the word means? Write your idea.

   **expression:** _____

   _____

2. Write a sentence with the word **expression**. Show what it means.

   _____

   _____

3. Check the meaning of **expression** in the Student Dictionary.

4. If your sentence in question 2 matches the meaning, put a ✓ after it. If your sentence does not match the meaning, write a better sentence.

   _____

   _____

5. Make a simple drawing to show the meaning of **expression**.

Academic Vocabulary Practice • Grade 4 • CD-104809

# Explore a Word

Read the sentences. Think about the meaning of each **bold** word. Then, check the Student Dictionary.

> The hills in the painting are **rhythmical** curves in a repeating pattern.
>
> Jazz musicians start with known songs and then **improvise** as they play, creating something new.

Complete the charts to show your understanding of the words *rhythmical* and *improvise*.

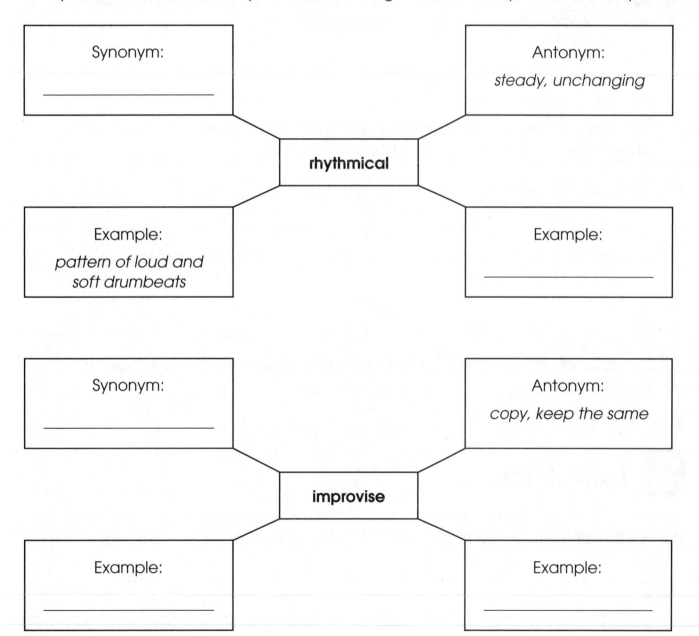

Synonym:
_____

Antonym:
*steady, unchanging*

**rhythmical**

Example:
*pattern of loud and soft drumbeats*

Example:
_____

Synonym:
_____

Antonym:
*copy, keep the same*

**improvise**

Example:
_____

Example:
_____

# Compare Words

Read the paragraph. Think about the meaning of each **bold** word. Then, check the Student Dictionary.

> The dancer stood in a stiff **posture**. As the music began, she slowly moved her arm in a welcoming **gesture**.

Complete each sentence with your own ideas about postures and gestures.

1. Sarah played the role of the queen in the play. Her posture was tall and straight. When she spoke to her servants, she made a gesture _____

   _____

   _____ .

2. Matt played the role of a servant in the play. He made a gesture of holding his palms together and bowing his head. His posture was _____

   _____

   _____ .

3. The dancer's posture expressed a feeling of sadness. His gestures were _____

   _____

   _____ .

4. The actor did not say a word. But, his posture and gestures showed anger. For example, he _____

   _____ .

## 🔍 Look It Up!

Is the first part of *gesture* pronounced like *jest* or like *guest*? Use the pronunciation in the Student Dictionary to answer the question. Explain how you know you are right.

_____

_____

# Compare Words

Read the paragraph. Think about the meaning of each **bold** word. Then, check the Student Dictionary.

> Would you like to paint a **watercolor**? With thin paint called *watercolor*, you can show one color under another. You can make the colors flow and blur together. Work fast, because watercolor dries quickly. You might prefer to paint a **pastel**. With chalk-like crayons called pastels, you can blend colors on the paper with your finger.

Circle the word in parentheses that completes each sentence.

1. The artist used short, quick brushstrokes to show the leafy trees in this (watercolor/pastel).

2. The artist held the soft green chalk. Using it like a pencil, she made curved lines. In the finished (watercolor/pastel), the lines look like waves on water.

3. Artists sometimes choose (watercolor/pastel) because they want the paper to show through the paint.

4. The colors in a (watercolor/pastel) can rub off. Artists usually spray a glue-like material on the finished work to fix the colors in place.

5. The different strokes used in some styles of (watercolors/pastels) can make the artwork look like colorful oil paintings.

6. When you view a (watercolor/pastel), look for the liquid, flowing qualities of the paint.

# Make Connections

Read the paragraph. Think about the meaning of each **bold** term. Then, check the Student Dictionary.

> An artist draws a scene on a flat sheet of paper, which is **two-dimensional**. Yet, the scene seems to have depth, length, and width. The scene looks **three-dimensional**. The artist has created **perspective** to show space and distance.

Underline the correct ending to each sentence.

1. The house in Picture 1 is
    A.   two-dimensional.
    B.   three-dimensional.

2. Angled lines turn a flat house into a house that seems
    A.   two-dimensional.
    B.   three-dimensional.

3. Picture 2 shows a tree drawn smaller than the house because
    A.   the artist is showing perspective.
    B.   a two-dimensional tree is smaller than a house.

4. Picture 2 is made on
    A.   two-dimensional paper.
    B.   three-dimensional paper.

5. Artists use perspective to make
    A.   three-dimensional shapes look flat.
    B.   two-dimensional shapes look as if they have depth.

# Make Connections

Read the paragraph. Think about the meaning of each **bold** word. Then, check the Student Dictionary.

> The artist is drawing a **portrait** of a boy. She views the boy from the side, because this portrait is a **profile**. She adds **shading** to the boy's cheek to show that it is round. She adds a **background** of a beach, even though she is painting indoors.

Complete each sentence. Include the vocabulary word in your answer.

1. profile
   If you look at the face on a dime, you will see _____

   _____ .

2. background
   When you view a painting or a drawing, you see _____

   _____ .

3. portrait
   A landscape shows an outdoor scene, but _____

   _____ .

4. shading
   In the real world, light and shadow fall differently on objects, so artists _____

   _____ .

 **Challenge!**

On a separate sheet of paper, draw a picture to illustrate each of the vocabulary words on this page. Label each drawing with the vocabulary word.

Name _____

# Make Connections

Read the sentences. Think about the meaning of each **bold** word. Then, check the Student Dictionary.

> Maria planned a **mosaic**. She arranged small colored tiles to make a design.
>
> Stephen cut out a **stencil** to print a repeating design.
>
> Cody made a **collage** of paper, feathers, and ribbon glued to a sheet of cardboard.
>
> The whole class painted a **mural** on a concrete wall outside the school.

Underline the correct ending to each sentence.

1. You often can see a mosaic on
    A.   the floor of a public building.
    B.   the roof of a tall building.

2. The place to see a mural is
    A.   outdoors.
    B.   on a wall.

3. A collage is interesting to look at because
    A.   of the different materials used.
    B.   of the unusual use of color.

4. When you make a print using a stencil, you
    A.   cut a design into wood or another material.
    B.   brush paint or ink through a hole.

5. Stencils are often used to
    A.   decorate walls and wooden furniture.
    B.   make a plan for a mural.

6. A mosaic collage is probably made of
    A.   bits of paper glued to a larger paper.
    B.   paper folded into three-dimensional shapes.

# Make Connections

Name _____

Read the paragraph. Think about the meaning of each **bold** word. Then, check the Student Dictionary.

> Actors read **scripts** to learn their lines. They note each **cue** that tells them when to enter or exit the stage. They learn when to sit or stand and how to handle each **prop** on the **set**.

Circle *Yes* or *No* for each question. Write your reason on the line.

1.  Could a cue be something a character says?                          Yes       No

    _____

2.  Could a play have more than one set?                                Yes       No

    _____

3.  Is the set the same as the scenery?                                 Yes       No

    _____

4.  If a character holds a flashlight, is the flashlight a cue?          Yes       No

    _____

5.  Do actors use scripts when performing?                              Yes       No

    _____

6.  Could a chair on a stage be a prop?                                 Yes       No

    _____

 # Word Alert!

The word *prop* is a shortened form of the longer word *property*, as in the term *theatrical property*. Use what you know about the words *theatrical* and *property* to explain the longer term.

_____

_____

# Make Connections

Read the paragraph. Think about the meaning of each **bold** word. Then, check the Student Dictionary.

> The musicians in an **orchestra** follow the signals of the **conductor**. The largest section of instruments is the **strings**. Violins, violas, cellos, and basses make up this section. The **woodwind** section usually includes flutes, oboes, clarinets, and bassoons. The **brass** section has trumpets, French horns, trombones, and tubas. Drums and cymbals are some of the instruments in the **percussion** section.

Label each picture with a vocabulary word.

1.

_____

2.

_____

3.

_____

4.

_____

5.

_____

6.

_____

Use the words *conductor* and *orchestra* in a sentence that tells about a musical performance.

7. _____

_____

# Play with Words

## Code Words

Choose the word or words that complete each sentence. Circle the letter.

1. Waving a fist is a ___.
   a  script
   b  prop
   c  gesture

2. Look for the tile pattern in a ___.
   q  posture
   r  mosaic
   s  watercolor

3. Stand up straight to show good ___.
   c  set
   d  script
   e  posture

4. An orchestra has ___.
   a  strings
   b  murals
   c  textiles

5. A sculpture is ___.
   t  three-dimensional
   u  perspective
   v  textile

6. A gesture is ___ of feeling.
   h  a posture
   i  an expression
   j  a perspective

7. A person or an animal is in ___.
   t  a stencil
   u  a collage
   v  a portrait

8. A knitted scarf is ___.
   d  a pastel
   e  a textile
   f  a loom

Write the circled letters in order. You will find a word that describes the arts.

_____

# Play with Words

## Letter by Letter

Choose the word that fits with each clue. Write it letter by letter. Some letters will be inside circles.

| | | | | |
|---|---|---|---|---|
| background | brass | conductor | perspective | script |
| shading | stencil | stencil | watercolor | woodwind |

1. Shows space and distance    _ _ _ _ _ _ _ _ _ ◯ _

2. A flute or an oboe    _ _ _ _ _ ◯ _ _

3. A print from a cutout    ◯ _ _ _ _ _ _

4. A leader with a baton    _ _ _ _ ◯ _ _ _ _

5. A tuba or a trombone    _ _ ◯ _ _

6. A design cutout    _ _ _ _ _ _ ◯

7. Use of darker line or color    _ _ ◯ _ _ _ _

8. What looks distant    _ _ _ _ _ ◯ _ _ _ _

9. A kind of painting    _ _ ◯ _ _ _ _ _ _ _

10. A play in print    _ ◯ _ _ _ _

Write the circled letters in order. You will find the answer to this question: *What is the name for painting, drawing, sculpture, collage, and photography?*

_ _ _ _ _ _    _ _ _ _

# Game Ideas and Suggestions

Use games and activities to help students better hear, see, and remember content-area vocabulary words. The suggestions on these pages can be used with the words in this book and with any other vocabulary words that students are learning.

## Charades

Choose about 10 vocabulary words. Write the words on slips of paper and display them. Give students time to think about the words before removing the slips. Then, divide the class into two teams. One team member chooses a slip, holds up fingers to indicate the number of syllables, and pantomimes the word. Teammates try to guess the word within a certain time limit.

## Word Art

Help students select vocabulary words to depict as art. Encourage them to use letter shapes and arrangements to indicate what the words mean. Prompt students with questions such as "How might you draw the letters of the word *three-dimensional*?" "Could you position the words *Arctic* and *Antarctic* to show their relationship?" or "What might happen to the letters in *erosion*?"

## Vocabulary Bingo

Reproduce and distribute the Vocabulary Bingo game card on page 105 for each student. Display a list of 40 vocabulary words and have each student choose 25 words to write on his or her card. Write each of the 40 words on a separate slip of paper. Shuffle the slips and choose one slip at a time. Instead of reading the word aloud, offer a clue about it. For example, for the word *insulator*, you might name the content area. "This is a science term that has to do with energy." Or, use a strong context sentence with "blank" for the word: "The 'blank' is wrapped around the wire that conducts electricity." Students should check off the word if it is on their grids. The first student to complete four across, down, or diagonally says "Bingo" and reads aloud the four words.

## Hink-Pinks

A *hink-pink* is a pair of rhyming words that answer a silly riddle. Use vocabulary words in the riddle and have students, individually or in pairs, come up with the hink-pink reply. Encourage students to review their vocabulary lists and write their own hink-pink riddles for classmates. Examples of riddles:

• What do you call *judicial* candy? (judge fudge)

• What do you call a lovely *glacier*? (nice ice)

• What do you call a place for *magma*? (a hot spot)

## Card Pairs

Use index cards cut in half to prepare a deck of 52 cards. Write 26 vocabulary words and 26 synonyms or short definitions on the cards. The cards can be used in a variety of games such as Memory or Concentration. Following is one suggestion.

# Game Ideas and Suggestions

- **Go Fish!** for 2 to 5 Players
- Each player is dealt five cards. The remaining cards are placed facedown in a pile.
- The player to the right of the dealer starts by setting aside any pairs. Then, she asks the player on the right for a card needed to make a pair. "Do you have *tundra*?" or "Do you have the meaning of *tundra*?"
- If the holder has the requested card, he or she hands it over. If the holder does not have it, the player must "go fish" and draw the top card from the pile. If no match can be made, the next player takes a turn.
- The winner is the first player with no cards in hand or the player with the most pairs after all cards have been drawn.

## Word Hunt

Emphasize that vocabulary words appear in print and online in a variety of informational resources. As you come across a vocabulary word—in a headline, a news article, an advertisement, or another resource—save the printed source or make a printout. Challenge students to read the text to find the vocabulary word and to explain what it means in the provided context.

## Dictionary Guess

Have one student randomly choose a word from the Student Dictionary and read the definition aloud to the class. Partners or small groups then try to write the vocabulary word that matches the definition. Continue until each student has had a chance to choose a word and read its definition aloud. Award a point for each correct word.

## Racetrack Games

Have students design their own racetrack board games or make one from a template you provide, such as the template on page 106. Here is one way to use the template:

- Select 25 vocabulary words for students to write in the spaces.
- Make a small cardboard spinner by drawing a circle divided into three sections labeled, 1, 2, and 3. The "spinner" can be a paper clip attached to a paper fastener.
- Provide small objects for students to use as markers.
- Each player spins, and player with the highest number goes first.
- The player spins and moves the marker the number of spaces shown. The player must say the word on the space and demonstrate knowledge of it by giving its definition or using it in a good context sentence.
- Players may use a dictionary to check the player's response. A player who is not correct loses a turn.
- The first player to reach the finish line wins.

| B | I | N | G | O |
|---|---|---|---|---|
|   |   |   |   |   |
|   |   |   |   |   |
|   |   |   |   |   |
|   |   |   |   |   |
|   |   |   |   |   |

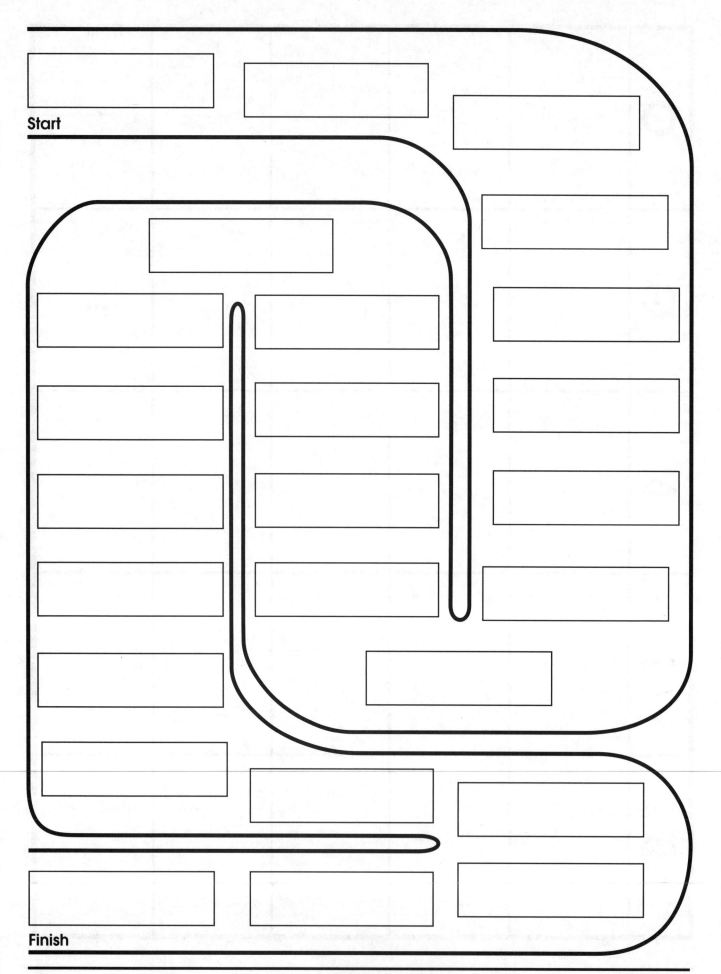

**Start**

**Finish**

Academic Vocabulary Practice • Grade 4 • CD-104809

# Student
# Dictionary

| | | | |
|---|---|---|---|
| a | bat | oi | **oil** |
| ā | day | o͞o | **too** |
| â | share | o͝o | **took** |
| ä | father | ou | **out** |
| e | net | u | **up** |
| ē | me | û | **fur** |
| i | big | th | **th**ink |
| ī | time | *th* | **th**at |
| o | hot | zh | treasure |
| ō | go | ə | happen, robin, lemon, circus |
| ô | for | | |

# Important Math Words I Need to Know

**bar graph** ('bär graf ) *noun phrase* A graph showing data with bars of different heights.

**center** ('sent ər) *noun* The point in the middle that is equidistant from all edges.

**centimeter** (sen' tə mē' tər) *noun* A unit of length equal to $\frac{1}{100}$ of a meter and about $\frac{2}{5}$ of an inch.

**circle graph** (sûr' kəl graf) *noun* A diagram, also called a *pie chart*, that shows a circle divided into sections, representing parts of a whole.

**circumference** (sûr kum' fər əns) *noun* The length of the boundary line of a circle.

**common denominator** (kom' ən di nom' ə nā' tər) *noun* A number that can be evenly divided by the denominators of two or more fractions. *The common denominator of the fractions $\frac{3}{4}$ and $\frac{3}{5}$ is 20.*

**convert** (kən 'vərt) *verb* To change over.

**cube** (kūbe') *noun* A figure that has six equal square sides.

**cubic unit** (kyōō' bik yōō' nit) *noun* A measure of volume, or the space within a solid form, based on how many cubes will fit inside.

**cylinder** (sil' in dər) *noun* A solid figure with two parallel circles at either base, or end

**diameter** (dī am' ə tər) *noun* A line segment between two points on a circle that passes through the center of the circle.

**equation** (i kwā' zhən) *noun* A number sentence with equal amounts on either side of the equal sign. *Example: 3 + 2 = 5*

**equivalent fractions** (i kwiv' ə lənt frak' shənz) *plural noun* Two or more fractions that show the same amount. $\frac{1}{2}$ , $\frac{2}{4}$ , and $\frac{50}{100}$ are *equivalent fractions.*

**face** ('fās) *noun* A flat surface on a geometric figure.

**factor** (fak' tər) *noun* A whole number that can divide another number without any remainder. *Factors of 12 include 1 and 12, 6 and 2, and 3 and 4.*

**frequency table** ('frē kwən sē 'tā bəl) *noun phrase* A table that shows a list of items and marks how often they occur with tally marks.

**horizontal axis** (hôr' ə zon' təl ak' sis) *noun* The line on a graph that goes from left to right,(also called the *x-axis).*

**improper fraction** ( im 'präp ər 'frak shən) *noun phrase* A fraction with a numerator that is equal to or larger than the denominator.

**inequality** (in'i kwol' ə tē) *noun* A number sentence with different amounts on either side of the greater than (>) or less than (<) sign. *Example: 3 + 2 > 4*

**kilometer** (kil' ə mē' tər or ki lom' ə tər) *noun* A unit of distance equal to 1,000 meters or about $\frac{5}{8}$ of a mile.

**line graph** (līn graf) *noun* A graph in which a line that rises, falls, or stays the same is used to show change over a period of time.

**mean** ('mēn) *noun* A middle point.

**median** ('mēd ē ən) *noun* The middle number in a list of numbers placed in order by value.

**mixed number** (mikst' nəm bər) *noun phrase* A whole number with a fraction.

**mode** ('mōd) *noun* the number that appears most often in a group of numbers.

**number sentence** ('nəm bər 'sen tən(t)s) *noun phrase* A mathematical expression that shows how numbers relate to each other.

**operation** (op' ə rā' shən) *noun* A series of steps taken to get a result. *Addition and subtraction are examples of operations.*

**percent** (pər sent') *noun* Parts of one hundred; hundredths.

**plane** (plān) *noun* A flat surface that stretches in all directions without end. *A tabletop is part of a plane. adjective* Describing a flat surface. *A square is a plane figure.*

**point of intersection** ('pȯint 'əv int ər 'sek shən) *noun phrase* The point where two lines cross.

# Important Math Words I Need to Know

**prism** (priz' əm) *noun* A solid figure with two matching ends, or bases. Each base is a shape made of three or more lines. The faces of a prism are four-sided figures with opposite sides that are parallel.

**probability** (prob' ə bil' ə tē) *noun* The chance that an event will occur, stated as a fraction. *The probability that a tossed die will land on a particular side is $\frac{1}{6}$.*

**proper fraction** ('präp ər 'frak shən) *noun phrase* A fraction with a numerator that is less than the denominator.

**pyramid** (pir' ə mid) *noun* A solid figure with a flat base of three or more sides and triangle faces that meet at a point at the top.

**radius** (rā' dē əs) *noun* A line segment from the center of a circle to any point on the circle.

**range** ('rānj) *noun* The difference between the lowest and the highest number or amount.

**rounding** (round' ing) *noun* The act of raising or lowering a number to the nearest ten, hundred, thousand, and so on.

**solid** (sol' id) *noun* A shape that has length, width, and thickness. *A pyramid and a cone are both solids. adjective* Describing a shape that has length, width, and thickness. *A pyramid is a solid figure.*

**vertical axis** (vûr' ti kəl ak' sis) *noun* The line on a graph that goes up and down, also called the *y-axis.*

**volume** (vol' yo͞om) *noun* The measure of the space inside a solid figure.

# Vocabulary Notes

_____

_____

_____

_____

_____

_____

_____

_____

_____

_____

# Important Science Words I Need to Know

**carnivore** ('kär nə vō(ə)r) *noun* An animal that eats meat.

**chemical energy** ('kem i kəl en ər jē) *noun phrase* Energy that is a result of chemicals reacting to each other. *The food you eat creates chemical energy.*

**circuit** (sûr' kit) *noun* The path of an electric current.

**closed circuit** ('klōzd 'sər kət) *noun phrase* A circuit without interruption, around which an electrical current can flow.

**conductor** (kən duk' tər) *noun* A material that allows energy to pass through it. *Metals, such as gold and silver, are good conductors.*

**consumer** (kən 'sü mər) *noun* Someone who buys and uses goods.

**crater** ('krāt ər) *noun* A hollow or hole made by an impact.

**crust** (krust) *noun* The solid outer layer of Earth.

**decomposer** (dē kəm 'pō zər) *noun* A fungus or a bacteria that breaks down dead plants and animals.

**earthquake** ('ərth kwāk) *noun* The shaking or rolling of Earth's surface.

**electric current** (i lek' trik kûr' ənt) *noun phrase* The movement or flow of positive or negative electric charges.

**electric energy** (i 'lek tri kəl 'en ər jē) *noun phrase* When electricity creates heat, light, or motion.

**energy** ('en ər jē) *noun* The ability to do work; usable power.

**erosion** (i rō' zhən) *noun* The process by which rock and soil are moved from one location to another.

**erupt** (i rupt') *verb* To burst forth powerfully. *Some volcanoes erupt frequently.*

**fault** (fôlt) *noun* A break in Earth's crust in which rocks on opposite sides slide past each other.

**food chain** ('füd chān) *noun phrase* The links between all living things, showing how each needs to eat another for survival.

**fossil** (fos' əl) *noun* The signs or preserved remains of a living thing from thousands or millions of years ago. *The fossils of shells found in rocks show that the land was once under water.*

**frequency** (frē' kwən sē) *noun* The number of sound waves that pass a particular point each second.

**herbivore** ('(h)ər bə vō(ə)r) *noun* An animal that eats plants.

**igneous** (ig' nē əs) *adjective* Formed from molten rock that has cooled and hardened. *Some igneous rocks form from lava.*

**inner core** ('in ər 'kō(ə)r) *noun phrase* The most interior or center of the four main layers of Earth.

**insulator** (in' sə lā' tər) *noun* A material that slows or prevents the passage of energy from another material. *Rubber is a good electric insulator.*

**intensity** (in ten' si tē) *noun* The measure of the power of particular sound waves. *Sound waves with high intensity are loud.*

**lava** (lä' və) *noun* A form of molten rock that flows from a volcano.

**light energy** ('līt 'en ər jē) *noun phrase* A form of electromagnetic energy that we can see. *Some light energy comes from the sun.*

**magma** (mag' mə) *noun* Rock heated to extremely high temperatures below Earth's crust. Magma is molten, or melted by heat.

**mantle** (man' tl) *noun* The layers of Earth that lie between the crust and the inner regions that form the core.

**metamorphic** (met' ə môr' fik) *adjective* Formed from rock that has been changed by heat and pressure within Earth. *Marble is a metamorphic rock.*

**mineral** ('min (ə) rəl) *noun* A natural substance usually found in the ground.

# Important Science Words I Need to Know

**omnivore** ('äm ni vō(ə)r) *noun* An animal that eats meat and plants.

**open circuit** ('ō pən 'sər kət) *noun phrase* A circuit that does not have a complete path for a current to flow.

**organism** ('ȯr gə niz əm) *noun* A living thing that has or can develop the ability to function on its own.

**outer core** ('aůt r 'kō(ə)r) *noun phrase* The second-last layer of the four main layers of Earth. It is composed of nickel and iron.

**pitch** (pich) *noun* The level of how high or low a sound seems. The pitch of a sound depends on how quickly the sound waves are vibrating.

**producer** (prə 'd(y)ü sər) *noun* The beginning of a simple food chain such as plants.

**rock cycle** (rok sī' kəl) *noun* A series of stages in which one type of rock changes into another. The rock cycle is a way of explaining how rocks change over time.

**sedimentary** (sed ə men' tə rē) *adjective* Formed from rock made of layers of material that have hardened. *Limestone is a sedimentary rock.*

**sound energy** ('saůnd 'en ər jē) *noun phrase* Energy produced by sound vibrations as they travel, permitting us to hear.

**transform** (tran(t)s 'fȯ(ə)rm) *verb* To change in appearance.

**vibrate** (vī' brāt') *verb* To move back and forth very quickly.

**volcano** (vol kā' nō) *noun* An opening in Earth's crust through which molten rock, cinders, ash, and gases flow or burst out.

**volume** (vol' yo͞om) *noun* The loudness of a sound.

**wavelength** (wāv length) *noun* The distance between a point on one wave and a point in the same position on the next wave.

**weathering** (weth' ər ing) *noun* The action of wind, rain, ice, heat, and other forces on rocks. *Weathering breaks rocks apart.*

# Vocabulary Notes

_____

_____

_____

_____

_____

_____

_____

_____

# Important Technology Words I Need to Know

**complex machine** ('käm pleks mə 'shēn) *noun phrase* A combination of two or more simple machines used to make work easier.

**conservation** (kän(t) sər 'vā shən) *noun* The planned protection of something to prevent misuse or extinction.

**CPU** (sē pē 'yü) *noun* The data-processing part of a computer.

**data** ('dāt ə) *noun* The base of information in a computer.

**effort** (ef' ərt) *noun* The force applied to a simple machine. *It takes less effort to push a weight up a ramp than to lift it with muscle power.*

**electronic** (i lek' tron' ik) *adjective* Having to do with electric signals made by controlling the flow and direction of electric charges. *Communication over cell phones and the Internet depends on electronic systems.*

**force** ('fō(ə)rs) *noun* An influence that changes speed or direction.

**fossil fuel** ('fäs əl 'fyul) *noun phrase* Made up of centuries-old plant and animal matter. *Three forms of fossil fuel are natural gas, oil, and coal.*

**friction** (frik' shən) *noun* A force that works against or slows down an object's motion. *Objects slide on ice because an icy surface has less friction than a bumpy surface.*

**fulcrum** (fool' krəm) *noun* The point on which a lever pivots, or turns.

**geothermal energy** (jē ō 'thər məl 'en ər jē) *noun phrase* A type of energy found under Earth, such as hot lava from a volcano.

**gravity** (grav' i tē) *noun* The force of attraction between objects, such as Earth and the sun, and between Earth and objects on Earth's surface. *The weight of an object depends on the force of gravity that acts on it.*

**icon** (ī' kon') *noun* A small picture on a computer screen that represents a program or a task. *Computer icons should be simple and easily recognized.*

**lever** (lē' vər or lev' ər) *noun* A simple machine made of a bar that turns on a support and is used to lift loads. *A wheelbarrow is one type of lever.*

**load** (lōd) *noun* The weight, or force, of an object that is lifted by a simple machine.

**mechanical** (mi kan' i kəl) *adjective* Having to do with machines.

**memory** (mem' ə rē) *noun* The data and the instructions stored on a computer chip. *Random access memory, or RAM, enables the user of a personal computer to work with programs.*

**menu** (men' yoo) *noun* A list of options, or choices, displayed on a computer screen.

**motion** ('mō shən) *noun* The act of changing place or position.

**multimedia** (mul' tē mē' dē ə) *noun* A combination of sound, text, animations, photos, video, and graphics, and other media.

**natural resource** ('nach (ə-)r əl 'rē sō(ə)rs) *noun phrase* Something that is found in nature but used by people.

**nonrenewable** (non' ri noo' ə bəl) *adjective* Having to do with an energy source or a natural resource that cannot be replaced after it is used.

**processor** (pros' es' ər or prō' ses' ər) *noun* The part of a computer that controls, or processes, electronic information.

**renewable** (ri noo' ə bəl) *adjective* Having to do with an energy source or a natural resource that does not run out or that can grow again.

**resistance** (ri 'zis tən(t)s) *noun* A force that opposes or slows.

**simple machine** ('sim pəl mə 'shēn) *noun phrase* A simple tool used to make work easier.

**solar energy** ('sō lər 'en ər jē) *noun phrase* Energy that comes from the sun.

# Important Language Arts Words I Need to Know

**adjective** (aj' ik tiv) *noun* A word that describes a noun or a pronoun. *One cloud is dark.*

**adverb** (ad' vûrb) *noun* A word that describes a verb, an adjective, or another adverb. *He spoke very loudly.*

**agreement** (əgrē' mənt) *noun* A grammar rule that says the verb must match the number of subjects. *Correct: That boy eats fast. Incorrect: That boy eat fast.*

**antonym** ('ant ə nim) *noun* A word that means the opposite of another word.

**apostrophe** (ə pos' trə fē) *noun* A mark that replaces missing letters in a contraction (*don't*), shows ownership (*David's*), or shows the plural of numbers and letters (*three X's*).

**author's purpose** ('ȯ thərz 'pər pəs) *noun phrase* The author's reason for writing a book or an essay.

**compare and contrast** (kəm pâr' and kən trast') *verb phrase* To describe things that are alike and things that are different.

**character** ('kar ik tər) *noun* A person in a story, a book, or a play.

**draft** ('draft) *noun* A quick version from which a final work is made.

**essay** (es' ā) *noun* A short written work on a topic. An essay usually tells about the writer's experiences and viewpoint.

**idiom** (id' ē əm) *noun* A group of words or a saying that has a special meaning. *The idiom* on top of the world *means "feeling happy."*

**metaphor** (met' ə fôr') *noun* A kind of comparison in which one thing is said to be another. *Example: The moon is a silver coin.*

**mystery** (mis' tə rē) *noun* A kind of story that usually involves a crime or a puzzle that needs to be solved.

**opposite** ('äp ə zət) *adjective* As different as possible.

**outline** (out' līn') *noun* A list of ideas and information to include in a written work. *verb* To list plans for a written work.

**persuade** (pûr swād') *verb* To try to get others to agree with your viewpoint or to do what you ask.

**plot** (plot) *noun* The action in a story. A plot often begins with a problem, continues with attempts to solve the problem, reaches a high point where the problem is or is not solved, and then drops to a conclusion.

**plural** ('plu̇r əl) *adjective* A word whose form means more than one person, place, or thing.

**possession** (pə zesh' ən) *noun* Ownership. Nouns and pronouns can show possession or who owns or has something. *Examples: the boy's dog, the dogs' collars, their house.*

**prefix** (prē' fiks) *noun* A word part added before a word to change its meaning or change how it is used in a sentence. *Examples: misbehave, unbutton, replay.*

**pronoun** (prō' noun') *noun* A word that takes the place of a noun. *The words* I, he, you, her, it, *and* them *are examples of pronouns.*

**punctuation** (pungk' chōo ā' shən) *noun* The marks used to signal pauses and other information in a sentence. Marks of punctuation include commas, periods, and semicolons.

**research** (ri sûrch' or rē' sûrch') *noun* Asking questions and looking for information that will provide answers.

**root word** ('rüt 'wərd) *noun phrase* A base word with no affixes.

**setting** ('set ing) *noun* The background of a story.

**similar** ('sim (ə) lər) *adjective* Being like something else in many ways.

**simile** (sim' ə lē) *noun* A kind of comparison, using *like* or *as* that points out a similarity in things that are not usually thought of as alike. *Example: a stare as cold as an icicle.*

**singular** ('siŋ gyə lər) *adjective* A word whose form means one person, place, or thing.

# Important Language Arts Words I Need to Know

**subject** (sub' jekt') *noun* The part of a sentence that tells who or what. *The <u>girls</u> talked. That <u>phone</u> is small. <u>Time</u> went by.*

**suffix** (suf' iks) *noun* A word part added to the end of a word to change its meaning or change how it is used in a sentence. *Examples: happi<u>ness</u>, care<u>ful</u>, slow<u>ly</u>.*

**summarize** (sum' ə rīz) *verb* To tell only the most important parts of a story or the main ideas in an informational work; to sum up.

**suspense** (sə spens') *noun* Waiting with nervousness and excitement for the next events in a story.

**synonym** ('sin ə nim) *noun* A word that means nearly the same as another word.

**topic sentence** (top' ik sen' təns) *noun phrase* A sentence that states the main idea of a paragraph or a section. A topic sentence is often the first sentence of a paragraph.

# Vocabulary Notes

_____

_____

_____

_____

_____

_____

_____

_____

_____

_____

_____

_____

_____

_____

# Important Social Studies Words I Need to Know

**agreement** ('ə grē mənt) *noun* When two or more people share the same opinion.

**agriculture** (ag' ri kul' chər) *noun* The management of soil and raising of crops and livestock; farming.

**ally** (al' ī) *noun* A person, a group, or a nation that has joined with another for a shared purpose. *verb* (ə lī') To work together or to fight a shared enemy.

**ancestor** (an' ses' tər) *noun* A grandparent's parent or an earlier person from whom one is descended.

**artifact** ('ärt a fakt) *noun* A found object that tells something about the development of a former culture.

**bibliography** (bib l ē 'äg rə fē) *noun* A list of writings about a particular subject or author, or items by an author.

**colonist** ('käl ə nəst) *noun* A person who lives in a colony or takes part in founding one.

**compromise** ('käm prə mīz) *verb* When two parties each give up something to come to an agreement.

**conflict** (kon' flikt) *noun* **1.** A dispute or a lasting fight. **2.** A struggle between opposite feelings or beliefs. *verb* (kn flikt') To differ or disagree. *Our opinions conflict, but we can still be friends.*

**debate** (di bāt') *noun* A discussion in which opposing sides express their views. *verb* To give reasons for and against a plan or an opinion.

**diplomacy** (də 'plō mə sē) *noun* Ability to deal with others without causing friction or bad feelings.

**diplomat** ('dip lə mat) *noun* A person who has the ability to deal with others without causing friction or bad feelings.

**equality** (i kwol' i tē) *noun* The state of being equal and having the same rights as others.

**evaluate** (e' val yə wāt) *verb* To find the value of something.

**fact** ('fakt) *noun* Something that is real or that exists.

**found** (fownd) *verb* To set up for the first time. *Spain wanted to found settlements in Florida.*

**frontier** (frun tēr') *noun* The edge of a settled area of land beyond which is wilderness.

**game** (gām) *noun* Wild animals or birds that are hunted for food or sport.

**generation** (jen' ə ra' shən) *noun* **1.** All of the family members at the same level of descent from an ancestor. *Parents and children are two generations.* **2.** A period of about 30 years, the time between the birth of parents and their children.

**hardship** (härd' ship) *noun* A problem or a difficulty that causes suffering.

**heritage** (her' i tij) *noun* Ideas and things passed down over time. *Americans' musical heritage includes jazz and rock music.*

**hunter-gatherers** (hun' tər gath' ər ərz) *plural noun* People who find wild sources of food, either by killing animals or by collecting plants, roots, and fruits.

**independence** (in' di pen' dəns) *noun* Having self-government; not being ruled by another nation. *African colonies fought for independence from European rulers.*

**inhabitant** (in hab' i tənt) *noun* Someone who lives in a particular place. *The inhabitants of the island reach the mainland by boat.*

**integration** (in' ti grā' shən) *noun* The act of making a school, a park, a bus, or other public place open to people of all races.

**international** (in' tər nash' ə nəl) *adjective* Involving two or more countries. *Ten nations signed the international trade agreement.*

**irrigation** (ir' i gā' shən) *noun* The watering of crops using constructions such as ditches and pipes.

**liberty** ('lib ər tē) *noun* The condition of freedom and independence from another entity.

# Important Social Studies Words I Need to Know

**Loyalist** (loi' ə list) *noun* An American colonist who wanted the colonies to remain under British rule.

**majority** (mə 'jȯr ət ē) *noun* A number that is at least one more than half of a total.

**migration** (mī 'grā shən) *noun* The act of moving from one place to another.

**militia** (mi lish' uh) *noun* A group of citizens with special training to fight as soldiers when called upon.

**national** (nash'ə nəl) *adjective* Having to do with a country or a nation. *Every country has its own national flag.*

**nomadic** (nō mad' ik) *adjective* Moving from place to place in search of food; roaming.

**Patriot** (pā' trē ət) *noun* An American colonist who wanted the colonies to be free of British rule. *Patriots fought against British troops.*

**pioneer** (pī' ə nēr') *noun* The first settler in a region.

**population** (päp yə 'lā shən) *noun* The number of people living in an area.

**primary source** (prī' mer ē sôrs) *noun phrase* A diary, an account, a speech, a photograph, a letter, a document, or other material that gives information about a historical event from the viewpoint of people who were involved in it.

**protest** (prō' test) *noun* An objection to something. *Example: a protest against high taxes.* *verb* (prə test') To complain about or object to. *Voters signed a document to protest higher taxes.*

**reliable** (ri 'lī ə bəl) *adjective* Able to be depended upon.

**research** (rē 'sərch) *noun* A careful study to gather facts about a particular subject.

**secondary source** (sek' ən der' ē sôrs) *noun* A report, an article, a painting, or other material that gives information about a historical event based on research of that event.

**segregation** (seg' ri gā' shən) *noun* The act of setting one group apart from the main group, often based on race or gender.

**territory** (ter' i tôr' ē) *noun* **1.** An area of land. **2.** A region that belongs to the United States but is not a state.

**tradition** (trə dish' ən) *noun* A belief or a custom that is passed down from each generation to the next.

**treaty** (trē' tē) *noun* A formal agreement between nations.

**unreliable** (un ri 'lī ə bəl) *adjective* Not able to be depended upon.

**works cited** ('wərkz 'sīt əd) *noun phrase* A listing of the sources of information used to compile a book or a report.

# Important Geography Words I Need to Know

**adapt** (ə dapt') *verb* To change one's body, behavior, or way of life to live in a changed environment.

**Antarctic** (ant ärk' tik) *noun* The region that includes the southernmost ocean, the South Pole, and the continent of Antarctica.

**Arctic** (ärk' tik) *noun* The region that includes the northernmost ocean, the North Pole, and the northern parts of North America, Asia, and Europe.

**biome** (bī' ōm) *noun* A large area that has a distinct community of plants and animals. *Plants that have adapted to little rainfall are part of a desert biome.*

**canyon** (kan' yən) *noun* A narrow and deep opening in the earth, carved by a river or other running water. *At the bottom of the canyon, we looked up at the steep walls of rock on either side.*

**cardinal direction** ('kärd nəl də 'rek shən) *noun phrase* One of the main directions, either north, south, east, or west.

**compass rose** (kum' pəs rōz) *noun* The circular symbol on a map that shows directions, such as the points of a compass.

**conservation** (kon' sûr vā' shən) *noun* The protection and the management of natural resources, natural environments, and wildlife.

**degree** (di 'grē) *noun* A unit of measurement.

**delta** (del' tə) *noun* The land, often in the shape of a triangle, that forms at the mouth of a river. *The river carries soil that builds up to form a delta.*

**equator** (i kwā' tər) *noun* The imaginary circle that runs east–west to divide the globe into a northern half and a southern half.

**floodplain** (flud' plān') *noun* The flat land on either side of a river that floods when the river overflows.

**glacier** (glā' shər) *noun* A great mass of ice formed from snow that has fallen over many years. A glacier moves slowly over land.

**globe** ('glōb) *noun* A round model showing the geography of Earth.

**hemisphere** (hem'i sfĕr') *noun* Half of the globe. The globe has an eastern and a western hemisphere. It also has a northern and a southern hemisphere.

**latitude** (lat' i tōōd') *noun* The distance on the Earth's surface north or south of the equator, measured in degrees. Lines of latitude run east–west around the globe.

**longitude** (lonj' i tōōd') *noun* The distance on Earth's surface east or west of an imaginary line called the *prime meridian*, measured in degrees. Lines of longitude run north–south between the Poles.

**plateau** (pla' tō) *noun* A large area of high and fairly flat land.

**prime meridian** ('prīm mə 'rid ē ən) *noun phrase* The line used as a reference line from which longitude east and west is measured.

**region** (rē' jən) *noun* **1.** An area of Earth's surface with shared characteristics. Climate, landforms, or plant life are some of the characteristics of a region. **2.** Any area in which people share cultural elements such as language, religion, or practices.

**strait** (strāt) *noun* A narrow body of water that connects two larger bodies of water.

**swamp** (swomp) *noun* A low-lying land with trees, shrubs, and woody plants that are adapted to flooding. Swamps often develop near rivers and streams.

**tropics** (trop' iks) *noun* The region of Earth's surface between the two lines of latitude known as the Tropic of Cancer, which is north of the equator, and the Tropic of Capricorn, which is south of the equator.

**tundra** (tun' drə) *noun* The Arctic area between

# Important Geography Words I Need to Know

the treeline and the polar ice. The tundra has only low-lying plants, and the soil below the surface is permanently frozen.

**wetlands** (wet' landz') *noun* Low-lying land that is flooded for all or part of the year. *Swamps, marshes, and bogs are examples of wetlands.*

## Vocabulary Notes

_____

_____

_____

_____

_____

_____

_____

_____

_____

_____

_____

_____

_____

_____

_____

_____

_____

_____

_____

_____